Archaeology of

Mayūrbhañj

Updating Indian Archaeology, no. 1

Archaeology of *Mayūrbhañj*

Prof. Prabodh Kumar Mishra

D.K. Printworld (P) Ltd.
NEW DELHI-110015

Cataloging in Publication Data — DK

Mishra, P.K. (Prabodh Kumar), 1937-
Archaeology of Mayūrbhañj.
(Updating Indian archaeology; no. 1).
Includes bibliographical references (p.).

Includes index.
1. Archaeology — India — Mayurbhanj.
2. Archaeology — India — Orissa. 3. Mayurbhanj, India — Antiquities. I. Title. II. Series : Updating Indian archaeology; no. 1.

ISBN 81-246-0084-8

First Published in India in 1997

Published by:
D.K. Printworld (P) Ltd.
Regd. office : 'Sri Kunj', F-52, Bali Nagar
New Delhi - 110 015
Phones : (011) 545 3975, 546-6019; *Fax* : (011) 546-5926

Printed by : DP's Impressive Impressions, New Delhi - 110059

Preface

MAYŪRBHAÑJ, the leading princely state of Orissā before Independence, was under the rule of the Bhañja dynasty which had the peacock as its royal emblem. Mayūrbhañj's ancient name (in the epigraphs) was Khijjiṅga *maṇḍala* with capital at Khijjiṅgakoṭṭa, identified with modern Khiching. Another place which served as the capital from 1400 to 1803 was Haripur and this was before the Bhañjas shifted to Baripāḍā. During the period of British rule Mayūrbhañj experienced an enlightended administration. All official activities, visits, events, income and expenditure were notified in the official Gazette. From the standpoint of size, population, natural resources and royal status Mayūrbhañj was accorded the highest position among the feudatory states of Orissā. A serious attempt was made in the time of Śrīrāmcandra Bhañjdeo (1892-1912) to trace the origin and antiquity of the Bhañjas on the basis of archaeological evidence. Eminent archaeologists/Indologists of India were invited to help the state in this endeavour. The result was the publication of *Archaeological Survey of Mayūrbhañj,* Vol. I by N.N. Vasu in 1911. Subsequently, R.P. Chanda published a report on Khicing in 1924-25 in the Annual Issue of the Archaeological Survey of India. From 1927 to 1942 the state conducted a series of exploration and excavation followed by conservation work at Haripur, Khicing and other places. The Museums at Baripāḍā and Khicing were set up to preserve and exhibit important antiquities discovered by the State Department of Archaeology. A good library was set up to promote historical study and research. Mayūrbhañj became the premier state to sponsor and facilitate archaeological studies by deputing scholars for a Post-Graduate course in Ancient Indian History and Culture at Calcuttā University and then for further training in the Archaeological Survey of India.

In those days the Princely states were regarded as outside the British administered territory. For education and employment the people in the states suffered from much deprivation. The archaeological activities in Mayūrbhañj did not find opportunity for publication as the Orissā Government neither had a Department of Archaeology nor a Research Journal for publishing research articles or significant discoveries of historical value. Against such odds, Mayūrbhañj made only satisfactory progress in archaeological programmes through the staff of its own Department of Archaeology.

After Independence Mayurbhanj became a district of Orissā from 1949 and its Department of Archaeology merged with the State Department of Archaeology. The valuable library was shifted from Baripāḍā to Bhubaneswar to constitute the core of Orissa State Museum Library. The State Archaeologist of Mayurbhanj became the Superintendent of Archaeology, Orissa in class II status. The prospects of archaeology in Mayūrbañj was lost in the labyrinth of bureaucratic indifference and neglect. In 1983 A. Joshi, the curator of Orissa State Museum, published his Ph.D. thesis under the title *History and Culture of Khijjingakotta* (Delhi, Vikas Publication) on the basis of compilation of facts already known. He had no access to the original records of the State Secretariat. In 1986 Balaram Srivastav of Benaras Hindu University published a monograph on *The Art of Khiching* (New Delhi). Both the above-mentioned works brought to light the antiquities of Khicing while ignoring other important places of antiquarian interest. What was more unfortunate was that neither of the scholars cared to delve deep into the background of archaeology in Mayūrbhañj. They saw the forest covered with beautiful foliage and creepers, ignoring the trees. Renowned scholars like Paramānanda Acarya and K.C. Panigrahi had academic pursuits and areas of interest other than Mayurbhanj though they had a great opportunity to focus upon the archaeological wealth of their home state which had financed their education.

The present book is an attempt to search for the background of the monuments of Mayūrbhañj on the basis of Government records obtained from the Mayūrbhañj State Record Room and other sources. The incredible patience and meticulous care with which the original sources were collected by Mamata Bose (Mohapatra) deserve due recognition and praise. But for her single-minded pursuit and perseverance this monograph would not have seen the light of day. That she furnished all the records/data to me for arranging the facts hitherto unknown in a book form speak eloquently of her noble mind. The author is extremely thankful to Annada Prasanna Mohapatra, S.K.B. Narayana, Bishnu Prasad Mohapatra, Ajoy Kumar Mohapatra, Gopal Bose, Polly Bose, Pullar Bose, Gargi Bose, Prajna Rout, Sharmila Sinha, Satarupa Mukherji and Anshuman Mohapatra for the help they rendered in various ways to complete the book. The monograph is purported to reveal the unknown aspects of the archaeological finds of Mayūrbhañj. It should, therefore, be seen to mark the beginning of practical archaeology in Orissā. Its contribution thus, adds an important chapter to the study of Indian culture. The result is for everyone to evaluate in the light of the newly-discovered facts. It is a tribute to the archaeologists who discovered the monuments from a state of oblivion and preserved them for the posterity. The photographs were prepared by Vivek of M/s Bedi Studio, Baripāḍā with the permission of the authorities whose help is acknowledged with gratitude.

Prabodh Kumar Mishra

Contents

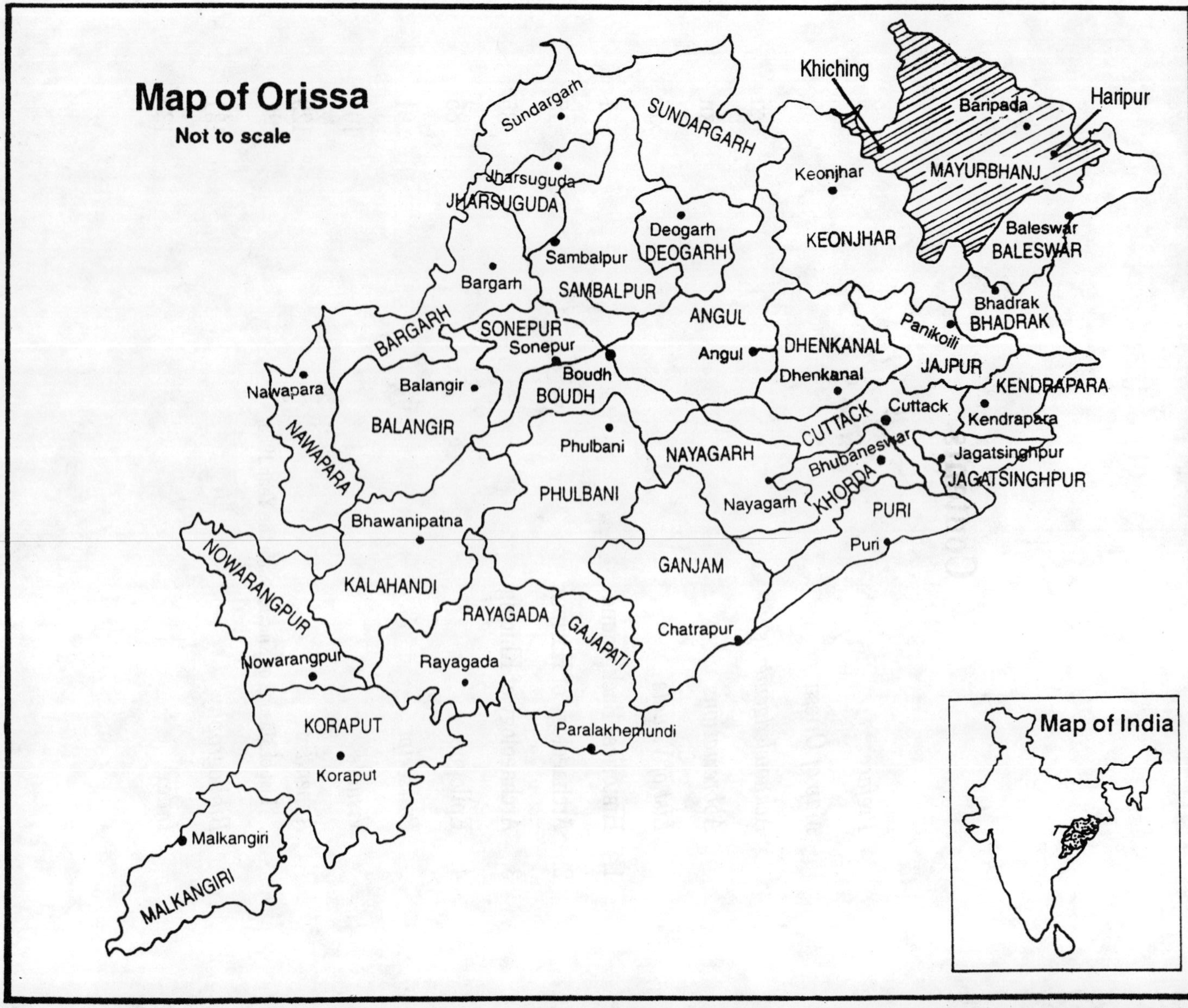
Map of Orissa
Not to scale
SUNDARGARH
Sundargarh
JHARSUGUDA
Jharsuguda
DEOGARH
Deogarh
SAMBALPUR
Sambalpur
BARGARH
Bargarh
SONEPUR
Sonepur
BOUDH
Boudh
ANGUL
Angul
KEONJHAR
Keonjhar
MAYURBHANJ
Baripada
Khiching
Haripur
BALESWAR
Baleswar
BHADRAK
Bhadrak
Panikoili
JAJPUR
DHENKANAL
Dhenkanal
KENDRAPARA
Kendrapara
CUTTACK
Cuttack
JAGATSINGHPUR
Jagatsinghpur
KHORDA
Bhubaneswar
PURI
Puri
NAYAGARH
Nayagarh
PHULBANI
Phulbani
BALANGIR
Balangir
NAWAPARA
Nawapara
KALAHANDI
Bhawanipatna
GANJAM
Chatrapur
GAJAPATI
Paralakhemundi
RAYAGADA
Rayagada
NOWARANGPUR
Nowarangpur
KORAPUT
Koraput
MALKANGIRI
Malkangiri
Map of India

Acknowledgements

THE records, documents, private papers and other archival sources of information were lying scattered and buried in the dust covered racks of the Mayurbhanj Collectorate Record Room, Jubilee Library, MPC College Library, State Museum Library, State Archives and various other places. The author is grateful to the following institutions and individuals for the assistance they rendered during the collection of data and oral evidence:

Dr. G.C. Chauley of the ASI, Bhubaneswar Circle; Staff of the Orissa State Museum and Orissa State Archives, Bhubaneswar; Sukdevmuni Dhal, Caretaker, Khiching Museum; Chaturbhuj Routray, Caretaker, Jubilee Library and Museum, Baripada; Maa Kichakesvari Yuva Kendra at Khiching; Priests and some distinguished persons of Khiching; Members of the Royal family (Rajmata Saheba Prem Kumari and Raj Kumari Prativa Manjari, Sri Pradip Chandra Bhanjdeo, the present Maharaja); Lal Saheb Pramod Chandra Bhanjdeo; Lal Saheb Bivas Chandra Bhanjdeo; Lal Saheb Nirmal Chandra Bhanjdeo; Govind Chandra Sahu, the Additional District Magistrate, Mayurbhanj; Susil Chandra Dash, Senior Advocate; Prasanna Kumar Dash, the Minister of Science, Technology and Environment; Harichandan Sahu and family of Sukruli; Gokul Chandra Das Adhikari and Pratap Chandra Bhanjdeo of Raruran; Kumudini Naik, Head Mistress, Pitabas Sahu; Laxminarayan Das; Prasanta Mahakud; Rajendra Mahanta; Kailas Chandra Khatua; Chandra Bhanu Naik and Anukul Naik of Khiching; Chandrasekhar Dey; Baikuntha Sethi and Raju; etc.

Abbreviations

ASI	: Archaeological Survey of India
ASIR	: *Archaeological Survey of India Report*
ASM	: Archaeological Survey of Mayurbhanj
IHQ	: *Indian Historical Quarterly*
JBORS	: *Journal of Bihar and Orissa Research Society*
ODG	: *Orissa District Gazetteers*
OHRJ	: *Orissa Historical Research Journal*
RAM	: *Annual Administration Report of Mayurbhanj*

List of Visuals

List of Plates

1

Historical Background

The Bhañjas

IN the medieval period the Bhañjas had established their political sway over two kingdoms, viz., Khiñjali *maṇḍala* in the Bauḍ-Phūlbānī region and Khijjiṅga *maṇḍala* in Mayūrbhañj. The former was ruled from Vañjulvaka and the latter from Khijjiṅga-koṭṭā identified with modern Khicing. These two kingdoms were located far apart from each other and had independent existence. The Bhañjas appear to have enjoyed local autonomy under the imperial suzerainty of the Bhauma-Karas (AD 736 to 940) whose era (the Bhauma era) was used in their epigraphs. The rise of the Somavaṁśī kingdom of Utkala in the second half of the tenth century led to the extinction of Khiñjali *maṇḍala*; but Khijjiṅga *maṇḍala* continued to survive for many more centuries as an independent sub-regional kingdom enriching Orissan history and culture in the tribal dominated region.

In the Copper Plate Inscriptions issued by the Bhañjas of Khiñjali and Khijjiṅga there is an identical account about their origin. Both the families claim Ādibhañja Vīrabhadra born out of the egg of a pea-hen as their progenitor. He was nourished and brought up by Sage Vasiṣtha at Koṭṭyāśrama, the hermitage. Koṭṭabhañja is another early ruler of the family who finds mention in the charters of both the groups. Peacock as the emblem of the Bhañjas has led scholars to believe that they were the scions of the Mauryas. In recent years modern account has linked up the Bhañjas of Mayurbhañj with one Rājpūt prince named Jaisingh.

Although the origin of the Bhañjas is shrouded in mystery and appears controversial and several families emerged with the suffix *bhañja* in the period of British rule (1803-1947), the erstwhile state of Mayūrbhañj enjoyed the benefit of Bhañja rule for an unusually long period of eleven centuries (850 to 1947) without any interruption.[1] The resultant political stability gave the Bhañjas an opportunity to contribute significantly to Orissan culture.

Mayurbhañj

At present Mayūrbhañj is a district in Orissā province. It lies between 21°17' and 20°34' North latitude and between 85°40' and 87°10' East longitude. The district covers an area of 6240 sq km of territory and is surrounded by Bengāl in the north, Bihar in the north-west, Keonjhar in the south and Balasore in the east. The area adjacent to Bālāsore and Bengāl is plain, whereas the rest of the land is covered by the hill range of the Eastern Ghāṭ. The people are mostly tribals consisting of 57 per cent of the total population.[2] Despite the tribal dominated population, the archaeology of the district appears to be quite rich.

The first evidence of man in the district is represented by the tools of the Lower Palaeolithic or Early Stone Age culture. On the banks of the river Budhābalanga and her tributaries like Sone and Gaṅgāhar the sites of this culture have been discovered. In this period of early history man was living close to the river where perennial water supply and animals of prey were available. He used ordinary stone tools made out of split pebble called flakes. Some of these tools have been discovered at Kuliānā. The typology of some of the tools are comparable to those found in the Sone valley. The crude pebble tools were used as handaxe, cleaver, scraper and knife, etc. It is interesting to note that in Mayurbhañj both flake and core tools were found together and the workmanship appeared to be mediocre.

The prevalence of Middle Stone Age culture is borne by the discovery of Stone implements in the Simlipāl hill range. These tools are small in size and made of flakes, and they consist of scrapers, borers, burins and points. A few well-made hand-axes and big hand points have also been found. The number of blades found appear to be quite large. These microlithic tools were hafted on wooden shafts and used as spears or arrowheads. The borers were used to pierce hides and skin and burins were helpful to engrave on wood. This period envisaged progress in technical skill. For making microlithic tools the raw material had to be of a very fine quality. Blade was a very popular tool. Wooden handles were often used for fixing the microlithic tools.

Mayūrbhañj is quite rich with regard to the discovery of Late Stone Age culture which witnessed polished stone celts. Baidipur and Kucai were the most flourishing Neolithic sites. At Baidipur the Neolithic settlement produced prehistoric pottery. The settlement was also associated with grinding and polishing of stone tools besides domestication of animals. The people were settled agriculturists and authors of early civilized life. They had crossed the stage of hunting and gathering food and had started a settled life of leisure and security, two basic requirements for the progress of civilisation.[3]

The name of the district can be explained by the fact that the Bhañjas who ruled over the kingdom had peacock (*mayūra*) as their royal emblem. Peacock is a sacred bird whose killing was prohibited. It is also believed that the combination of two medieval ruling families — Mayūras of Bonai *maṇḍala* and Bhañjas of Khijjiṅga *maṇḍala* — resulted in naming the areas as 'Mayūrbhañj'. This belief is corroborated by the fact that one Dharaṇī Varaha and his wife Kirtti had sculpted the colossal image of Avalokiteśvara Bodhisattva during the rule of King Rāya Bhañj in Khijjiṅgakoṭṭā sometime in the ninth century AD. The ancient name of 'Khijjiṅga *maṇḍala*' was discarded after shifting of the capital to Hariharpur (now called Haripur) in AD 1400 as a result of the depredations caused by Feroz Tugluq in AD 1361 and the new kingdom was called Mayūrbhañj. 'Peacock' substituted 'Bull' as the royal insignia of the Bhañja rulers of Haripur.[4]

Sources

The early history of Mayurbhañj is based on varied sources. At Baidipur, Kuliānā and Kucai the discovery of palaeolithic and neolithic tools provided evidence of the Stone Age culture. There are at least eleven copper plate charters issued by the Bhañja kings in the early medieval period which furnish information about religious and social history, besides an account of their origin.[5] These copper plate inscriptions have been dated in Bhauma era (AD 736) and this gives a clue to the period of their issue.[6] Valuable information is also furnished by the epigraphs on the genealogy of the family and the administrative organisation. The discovery of Roman coins, Kuṣāna coins and Gupta coins throw light on the trade, commerce and currency system of the period.[7] Historians believe that in the second and third centuries the Muruṇḍas (an Indo-Scythian tribe) were ruling over the region. The finding of Roman coins is a positive evidence of trade links with the Roman empire. The ancient port of Tāmralipti so frequently mentioned by foreign and Indian chroniclers was the route for the maritime trade of Khijjinga *maṇḍala*.[8]

Another authentic source of information about the early history of Khijjinga *maṇḍala* comes from the discovery of a large number of monuments scattered over a vast area in places like Ayodhyā, Bādaśāhī, Dhuduā, Gajariśāsan, Haripur, Khicing, Kanisāri, Koisāri, Kutting, Manināgeśvara, Mānitri, Porādihi, Purāngāo, Pathuriāgaḍa, Rānibandha and other places. The monuments and sculptures discovered in the above-mentioned places are of inestimable value to reconstruct the history and culture of ancient and early medieval Mayūrbhañj.[9] Apart from providing historical data, these monuments bear testimony of the evolution of Orissan art and temple architecture. Though a contemporary of Bhubaneśwar school of art, Khicing appears to be yet another centre which disseminated powerful and distinct artistic tradition in Orissa. Lying isolated in an inaccessible region, the art school of Khicing carried the banner of Bhubaneśwar tradition with equal vigour and multiplicity.

Discovery

The invasion of Orissā by Feroz Śāh in 1361 spelt disaster for the medieval township of Khijjiṅgakoṭṭā as the invaders destroyed the standing monuments forcing the kings to shift to a safer area away from the much frequented trade route taken by the Tugluq Sultan.[10] In 1400 Harihara Bhañja established his capital at Hariharpur, now known as Haripur, and the kingdom was called Mayūrbhañj. Khijjiṅgakoṭṭā and Khijjiṅga *maṇḍala* were forgotten in the limbo of history. The beautiful monuments of the Jains, Buddhists and Brāhmaṇical cults remained in darkness for almost five centuries coinciding with the changing political fortune of India. During this period, the Afghans of Bengāl, the Mughals and the Marāṭhās successively ruled over Orissā. Mayūrbhañj as a princely state during this period maintained a subordinate existence under the Paramount powers. In 1803 it came under the British paramouncy when Rājā Damodar Bhañja accepted the East India Company as his political overlord and signed treaties and engagements as a tributary chief.[11]

The first European who discovered the ruins of Khicing was Lieutenant Tickell whose memoir published in the *Journal of Asiatic Society*, Bengal (Vol. IV, pp. 706-09) revealed the antiquarian remains of the place and two temples lying hidden amidst the untrodden jungles. He writes

> In the dense forests of bushes and trees there lie scattered portions of elaborate sculptures, idols and figures of men in armour on horseback, *nauchnees* (dancing girls), jugglers and servants, etc. These two temples are part of a circle of sixty similar ones which with sixty corresponding tanks are placed two miles apart in a circle of forty miles in diametre.

This gives a dismal picture of Khicing in ruins as it appeared in 1840. In the *Archaeological Survey Report* of Cunningham, J.D. Beglar in 1874 and 1876 mentions Khicing as 'Kicang' and reports about the pillared hall, Vaiṣṇavite and Śaivite temples, Buddhist *stūpa*s, lifesize figure sculptures and the sacrificial remains of goats besides numerous large size bricks.

The accession of Mahārāja Śrīrāmcandra Bhañj Deo in 1892 was a turning point in the history of Mayūrbhañj. Like his father Kriṣṇacāndra Bhañj Deo (1867-1882), the new king was a liberal minded and enlightened ruler. He had availed of Western education and was a much travelled man. His tutor Mohinī Mohan Dhar, who subsequently became the Dewān of Mayūrbhañj, had been a guiding factor in the Mahārāja's career. Apart from administering the state with great care and foresight, the Mahārāja had developed a keen interest in literature, geology, irrigation and education. He was a true nationalist who assumed the leadership of the Utkal Union Conference in December 1903 as the President of the inaugural session held at Cuttack.[12] The unification of the scattered Oriyā-speaking people under one administration and a revival of their glorious past was quite dear to his heart. The visit of Lord Curzon to Orissā, to see the historical monuments at Bhubaneśwar, Purī and Koṇārka and the restoration of Koṇārka temple in 1900-01 as a mark of respect to Orissā's past must have created an indelible impression in the mind of young Śrīrāmcandra. He encouraged Bengālī intellectuals, scientists and jurists to come and settle down in Mayurbhañj for the development of the state. The appointment of P.N. Bose was inspired by the zeal to conduct a geological survey of the state for exploiting its mineral resources.[13] Likewise, his deep interest in the glorious heritage of the past motivated him to appoint the eminent Indologist Nāgendra Nāth Vasu in 1906 as the Head of the Archaeological Department to conduct an archaeological survey. N.N. Vasu writes :

> It was in 1906 that I had the pleasure of an interview with the Chief of Mayurbhanja and was struck with the earnestness and the spirit of devotion with which he espoused the cause of antiquarian research in Orissa. I was told that he had already commenced an archaeological enquiry under the auspices of which the work of exploration was being laboriously conducted within his jurisdiction.[14]

This 'uncommon interest' of the Maharaja to unearth the cultural heritage led to the publication of a scholarly work entitled *The Archaeological Survey of Mayurbhanj* by the State in 1911. This was the result of N.N. Vasu's archaeological exploration and investigations conducted in Mayūrbhañj during 1907-09. In the aforesaid volume Vasu discussed the religious history of Mayūrbhañj through the ages and also the archaeological importance of 45 sites. In the Appendix he analysed the contents of eight copper plate inscriptions issued by the Bhañjas and the Sulkis of Kodālakamaṇḍala.[15]

Vasu considered Khicing as of premier archaeological interest for the large number of monuments he witnessed there and their rich antiquarian value. He admits,[16] 'The superior workmanship of these have indeed been a startling discovery for us'. Vasu continues :

> The picturesque land bears its silent history of ages on its temples and

> images. Its record of archaeological glory has to be discovered from amongst the vast ruins overspreading it, some of which have long ceased even to see light and would have to be brought out again by excavators.[17]

The prophesy of Vasu came true in the pioneering works done by Kāmākṣyā Prasād Bose, the Sub-Divisional Magistrate of Pañcapīr during the first decade of the present century.

II

Mahārāja Śrīramcandra Bhañj Deo (1892-1912) was an enlightened ruler who introduced several measures of reforms while organising the administrative structure and initiating welfare measures. He divided the state to four sub-divisions : Sadar, Pañcapīr, Bāmanghāṭy and Kaptipadā. Except the Sadar, the other three sub-divisions were adminstered by sub-divisional officers with magisterial power and having the status of Chief Executives.[18] Such key administrative posts were held by highly educated persons who proved their worth by wisdom and experience. The Dewān of Mayurbhañj who assisted the Mahārāja to modernise the State adminstration was Mohini Mohan Dhar,[19] the private tutor of the ruler when the latter was a student of Ravenshaw College, Cuttack. Since his assumption of the office of Dewān in 1904 Mohinī Mohan played a major role in selecting the right type of persons for responsible posts. He was actually the conscience-keeper of the Mahārāja. Kāmākṣyā Prasād Bose and Jatindra Mohan Dhar were two promising Law Graduates of Calcutta University whom Mohinī Mohan had inducted into state service.

It was in the eventful year of 1905 when Bengāl was partitioned by the British Government on communal considerations that the Hindu elites of East Bengāl (now Bangladesh) received a serious jolt in their socio-political life. The Swadeśī Movement following the partition created a new stir of nationalism, the fire of which caught Bengāl as never before. In this situation Mayūrbhañj gained the services of the aforesaid two young Bengālī intellectuals — Kāmākṣyā Prasād Bose and Jatindra Mohan Dhar. Kāmākṣyā Prasād Bose was the son of Kāśīnāth Bose, a prominent zamīndār of East Bengāl near Dacca. After passing matriculation from the local High School he did his graduation from Calcutta

University in 1898. He took the Law Degree from the same University two years later and started legal practice at the Dacca High Court. In 1905 he joined as a Magistrate-cum-Deputy Collector in Mayūrbhañj. He and Jatindra Mohan served Mayurbhañj as top civil servants to fulfil the aims of the Maharaja. After being appointed as Deputy Collector, Baripāḍā, Kāmākṣyā Prasād was soon promoted as Assistant-Sub-Divisional Officer and then as Sub-Divisional Officer in a short period of two years. He had the opportunity to serve as the Sub-Divisional Officer of Pañcapīr, Bāmanghāṭī and Kaptipada successively and was considered by the Maharaja as a very efficient officer of high integrity. He took keen interest in the economic development of the state by encouraging cottage industries and exploiting the natural resources.[20]

Kāmākṣyā Prasād was influenced by the nationalist urge for Swadeśī. The Utkal Union Conference inaugurated by Mahārāja Srīrāmcandra for uniting the scattered Oriyā-speaking people and improving their economy had also suggested industrial growth at the village level besides the introduction of scientific methods of agriculture. During the annual session from 1903 to 1919 the Conference repeated the resolution to improve the economic condition of the Oriyās through professional education, industrial undertakings, better methods of agriculture to augment production and promotion of cottage industries.[21] In response to the needs of the time Kāmākṣyā Prasād observed the vast potentiality of sericulture in Mayurbhañj. While he was the Sub-Divisional Officer of Bāmanghāṭī he brought a few weavers' families from East Bengāl and settled them at Bahaldā. Through them he spread the technique of sericulture and weaving of tassar clothes among the local people.[22] Having realised the prospects of rich forest wealth he advised the State Government to encourage the production of wax. He assisted in the establishment of two Lac factories in the Bāmanghāṭī Sub-division.[23] To improve the quality and methods of production of articles he trained a body of artisans. To provide the much needed expertise for gradual industrial growth he started a Technical School at Baripāḍā in the pattern of a Polytechnic Institute. Organisation of agricultural and industrial exhibition became an annual feature in the state to disseminate new knowledge among the people and to give award to ideal producers. The Sericulture of Mayurbhañj received accolade in the exhibition held at Calcutta, Jaipur and

Bālāsore in 1906, 1910 and 1911 respectively.[24]

As an efficient administrator he had received special commendation from the Mahārāja for having settled the boundary disputes between Mayūrbhañj and Kaptipaḍā.[25] He had completed the survey work in the inaccessible Similipāl region (Durgādihā-Podādihā) by strenuous work of over three months. In recognition of his merit he was bestowed with special magisterial powers by the Mahārāja.[26]

He was considered to be a most efficient Superintendent of the State Jails and in that capacity he discharged responsibility in all the three Sub-divisions (Pañcapīr, Bāmanghāṭī and Kaptipaḍā).[27] He served as Special Judicial Officer of Baripāḍā, Special Revenue Officer, Sadar Sub-division and as the Deputy Collector, Sadar.[28] As a philanthropist he organised Relief works for the distressed people of Bāmanghāṭī and helped them with food and money. He raised relief fund through public contribution.[29] He was quite judicious and prompt in dispensing justice.[30]

During his tenure as the Sub-Divisional Officer of Pañcapīr he revived the religious importance of Khicing by organising an annual festival on the occasion of *Śivacaturdaśī* (February-March). The week-long festival gave the people an opportunity to visit the religious shrines at Khicing and to sell and purchase articles of local produce and needs. People from far and near used to flock there in their colourful tribal costume and celebrated with dance and music as well. The *melā* is organised even today.

The greatest contribution of Kāmākṣyā Prasād was the discovery of the archaeological treasures of Khicing during his tenure as the Sub-Divisional Officer of Pañcapīr Sub-Division in 1907. The establishment of the Department of Archaeology under the stewardship of Nāgendra Nāth Vasu[31] in 1905-06 and the posting of Kāmākṣyā Prasād to Karañjia, the Sub-Divisional Headquarters, was a strange coincidence. Kāmākṣya Prasād during his studentship in Calcutta University had shown a flare for historical studies. In Mayūrbhañj he must have received patronising support from the Mahārāja whose nationalist zeal and antiquarian interest was too well-known. The story goes that Kāmākṣyā Prasād accidentally came across a buried image of Avalokiteśvara and arranged for its excavation.[32] The story reveals that while washing his hands after lunch at a place he noticed that the water was not passing through the soil. With uncanny curiosity of an antiquarian he got the place dug and the result was the amazing discovery of the image. The image had an epigraph which read as *oṁ rājye śrī rāyabhañjasya lokeśo bhagavānayam śrī dharaṇī varahenasaha kīrttya vinirmitaḥ,* meaning thereby that the image was sculpted by Dharaṇī Varāha and his wife Kīrttī for the king Rāya Bhañja.[33] This epigraphic evidence was a clue to the date of the image and the historicity of Khicing. After Nāgendranāth Vasu identified Khijjiṅgakoṭṭā of the eighth century with modern Khicing the curiosity of Kāmākṣya Prasād for historical quest knew no bounds.[34] He had long forgotten Dhamrāi of East Bengāl, his birthplace and has developed a strong fascination for Mayūrbhañj as his new homeland. The discovery of Avalokiteśvara image unfolded before him the vision of an ancient kingdom and people enriched by a glorious cultural past. He plunged headlong in extending his historical knowledge about ancient Khijjiṅgakoṭṭā by undertaking archaeological exploration and excavation.[35] While Nāgendra Nāth conducted a general survey and exploration of Mayūrbhañj, Kāmākṣyā Prasād devoted himself to an in-depth study of the archaeological treasures he discovered at Khicing.

Before we deal with the monuments and priceless antiquities which Kāmākṣya Prasād brought to limelight it would be proper to make a general study of the religious history of Khijjiṅga *maṇḍala* on the basis of epigraphic and archaeological evidence.

The Bhañja rulers were devotees of Śiva. In their official records they have described themselves as 'Paramamāheśvara' and the copper plates bear the Śaivite emblem 'bull'. They had built a number of Śaivite shrines most of which are no more. Some structural remains may be seen at Khicing in the form of ruins of Khaṇḍiyāḍeulā, Kutaituṇḍi, etc. The Bhañja king Pṛthvībhañjadeva was the worshipper of Hara and this image has been preserved in the Khicing Museum.[36] The discovery of several Umā-Maheśvara images also prove the Śaivite leanings of the Bhañjas.

That they were devotees of Śakti is borne by the fact that Khijjiṅgeśvarī or

Cāmuṇḍā was the tutelary deity of the Bhañja dynasty. The presiding deity of Khicing was Cāmuṇḍā. Several images of Durgā Mahisamardinī and Saptamātṛkās bear evidence of the popularity of Śāktism.[37]

The mention of 'Bhava' in the copper plate grants may suggest that Sūrya was highly venerated by the Bhañjas. Bhava is one of the names of Sūrya as found in the list of twelve Ādityas. The discovery of several Sūrya images indicate the popularity of Sun worship in Khijjiṅgakoṭṭā. The worship of Dikpālas and Navagrahas was also prevalent there.

Although there is no epigraphic evidence for the Bhañjas' inclination towards Vaiṣṇavism, the remains of a ruined Viṣṇu temple and some beautiful images of the God are adequate proof of the presence of Vaiṣṇavism and the tolerant attitude of the ruling family.

The worship of Ganapati was another aspect of the religious history of Khijjiṅgakoṭṭā. Several images of Gaṇeśa have been found there.[38]

From the above discussion it may be concluded that Khijjiṅga-koṭṭā was a centre of *pañcopāsana* where five most popular Hindu cults enjoyed a flourishing status. These cults centred round Śiva, Durgā, Gaṇeśa, Bhāskara and Viṣṇu. But that was not all. The people there included the followers of Nāga cult also. Serpent Goddess Manasā was worshipped in anthropomorphic form. Half human and half serpent figures of the goddess were also used as objects of worship. The legendary family called Virāṭa-Bhujaṅgas who preceded the Bhañjas had accepted 'Nāga' as their tutelary deity.[39] In view of the tribal composition of the population, worship of 'totems' and serpents was the normal feature of religious life. The Āsanpaṭ Inscription of King Śatrubhañja mentions the powerful king as a member of the Nāga family (*Nāganvaya*).[40]

There was probably a political alliance between the Virāṭa-Bhujaṅga family and the Bhañjas, and the fusion between them resulted in the acceptance of serpent worhsip at Khijjiṅgakoṭṭā. This is corroborated by the presence of a Nāga-Nāginī temple in the south of Khicing.[41]

Khicing was also a centre of heterodox faiths. The Itāmundiā site is full of

Buddhist antiquities which have yielded a number of images of Maricī. Kings like Rāya Bhañja or Rāja Bhañja were Buddhists and ardent worshippers of Avalokiteśvara, a very popular Mahāyānic deity. There are fine Buddha images in *bhūmiśparsa mudrā*. One such image was found from a ruined brick structure which was probably a Buddhist monastery.[42] The mound called Itamuṇḍiā was excavated by Kāmākṣyā Prasād Bose in 1908.[43] Other Mahāyānic and Vajrayānic images of Maricī, Mañjuśrī and Tārā have also been found datable to tenth-eleventh centuries. These are beautiful specimens of art.[44] It appears that in the twelfth century Tāntric Buddhism had prevailed in Khicing. Several images of Vajra-Tārā, Kurukullā, and Aparacana Mañjuśrī discovered there prove this hypothesis.

In the last phase of Khijjiṅgakoṭṭā before its destruction by the Muslim invaders, Jainism enjoyed a flourishing status. This is indicated by the discovery of the images of Jaina Tīrthaṅkaras, viz. Ṛṣabhanātha, Śāntinātha and Pārśvanātha from the premises of Khaṇḍiaḍeulā.[45]

Thus, in Orissan culture, Khicing occupied a unique position. There is no other place which may vouch for such a claim. The coexistence of major Brāhmaṇical cults along with Buddhism and Jainism is not to be found anywhere else. This not only adds to the catholic attitude of the rulers who had ruled from Khicing for over five hundred years, but it is also a sure proof of the real nature of Orissan culture. Such extraordinary aspect of our cultural heritage could be revealed by the meticulous care and diligence of an administrator-archaeologist like Kāmākṣyā Prasād Bose. He laid the foundation of Archaeological Survey of Mayūrbhañj by his pioneering efforts during 1907-08.

The site locally known as the Saṅkuā Rājār Garh was excavated by Kāmākṣyā Prasād following the discovery of the inscribed image of Avalokiteśvara. In Mahāyāna Buddhism the concept of Bodhisattva led to the creation of the images of Vajrapāṇi, Padmapāṇi Avalokiteśvara, etc. Among the five Bodhisattvas, Avalokiteśvara enjoyed the highest popularity. From the primodial Buddha or *ādi* Buddha and *ādi* Prajña emanated five *dhyānī* Buddhas, namely, Akṣhobhya, Ratnasambhava, Vairocana, Amitābha and Amoghasiddhi. From these *dhyānī*

Buddhas emanated respectively five Bodhisattvas — Vajrapāṇi, Ratnapāṇi, Sāmantabhadra, Padmapāṇi-Avalokiteśvara and Viśvapāṇi. Among all these deities Avalokitesvara was the most popular one.

The Saṅkuā Rājār Garh site still has a chlorite door-jamb bearing the curving of a conch-chell. It appears to be a Vaiṣṇavite site. Not far away from the place is Itamuṇḍiā, a mound full of brick debris which has been ransacked by the villagers for ancient bricks for building houses. There is a stone door-jamb *in situ*, but in an upside-down position. It was not so when Bose undertook the excavation work. Itamuṇḍiā was a Buddhist site because the debris is believed to represent the vestiges of a monastery.

Bose undertook the excavation of a temple site called Dedhasura-Bhāibāhu on the right bank of the river Khairabhaṇḍan in 1908. Two beautiful images of Umā-Maheśvara now preserved in the local museum were unearthed here. The larger image was enshrined in a temple built of laterite foundation, whereas the smaller was recovered from a brick temple. The plinth, door-jambs and lintel of the brick temple are *in situ*.

Virāṭgarh was another important site which attracted the attention of Bose. In 1908 he excavated the central mound by taking a trial trench on the eastern side. The excavation led to the discovery of a ruined brick wall, a Kuṣāṇa coin, an earthen jar, and a small piece of gold besides a stone seal of the second century AD. Among the structural remains Bose discovered three rooms with verandah. Each room was 13 '6" x13 'size and the thickness of the wall was 5 '. The walls rose to a height of 6 'or more. The verandah in the east was 36 'long and 11 'wide with a staircase at the southern end. This building had an adjacent structure which could not be excavated. In all probability, the structure represented the vestiges of a Buddhist monastery.

Vāsulisāl was yet another archaeological site excavated by Bose in 1908. His archaeological spade also touched a small mound near the Ṭhakurānī's compound where a *Kaima* tree was being worshipped by the local people who referred to the area as 'Karamā rājār garh' (the fort of the Karamā King). On the occasion of the Karamā festival the people used to worship the tree. From the site, a small but beautiful image of Ardhanārīśvara was discovered by Bose.

Not far away from the Khicing village a site called Itamuṇḍiā drew the attention of Bose owing to its ruins of a brick structure. The clearance of the debris resulted in the discovery of a monastery, an inscribed image of Maricī, one Avalokiteśvara and Buddha in *bhūmiśparsha mudrā*. The inscribed Maricī image was shifted to Baripāḍā along with a small image of Mahiṣāsuramardinī which were sent to the exhibition on Indian Art held at London under the auspices of the Burlington Fine Art Club.[46] On palaeographical ground the inscription on the image of Maricī has been dated to tenth century[47] and the inscribed image of Avalokiteśvara to eleventh century.[48] An image of Tārā seated on a Lotus in *lalitāsana*, holding *Nīlotpala* in her left hand and showing *abhaya mudrā* in the right hand, and surrounded by flying Apsarās and Gandharvas was another significant discovery from the site. Her profusely ornamented body and head-dress and symmetrical delineation represent the typical art quality of Khicing.[49] The size of the image is 13" x 9½".

Among other discoveries and collections of Bose mention may be made of the images of Mahāvīra, (from Khicing, Kuāmārā and Bādaśāhī), Nāga (from Kuamara), Ambikā, Maricī and Gaṇeśa (from Kuāmārā), Umā-Maheśvara (from Kaisarigarh and Khicing), Nṛsiṁha (from Bādaśāhī), Garuḍa (from Agāriā), Ajaikapāda (from Kainsari), Avalokiteśvara (from Rānībandha near Bādaśāhī), Bhairava and Hara-Gaurī (from Khicing), an inscribed stone slab (from Pedagadi), Khaṇḍadeuli plate of Raṇa Bhañja,[50] Ukhunda Plate of Pṛthvī Bhañja[51] and many other antiquities of great artistic and historical value.[52]

Bose was a roving archaeologist. Wherever he went or served as an officer till his death in 1925, he kept a vigilant eye on the archaeological wealth of the state. The sudden demise of Mahārāja Srīrāmcandra Bhanj Deo in 1912 was a rude shock to his antiquarian pursuits. But by that time he had already carved out a place for Mayurbhañj on the map of Indian Archaeology. From Prehistoric tools to historical epigraphs and sculptures, he made a discreet collection and meticulously arranged for their preservation at the Site Museums at Khicing and Baripāḍa. The Accession Registers maintained by the Museum authorities mention categorically the antiquities collected by Bose, not forgetting to record the date and place of collection. His efforts unearthed the glorious cultural contributions of the Bhañjas in art and iconography. His life-long dedication to archaeological discovery and sound knowledge on the subject prompted him in 1922 to take Ramā Prasād Candā, an eminent archaeologist of India, round the state showing various sites and explaining their potentialities. His pioneering activites facilitated later scholars like Candā and Paramānand Ācārya to prepare a chronological account of the history of the Bhañjas of Mayurbhañj.[53]

The strenuous activities undertaken by him throughout his career as a dedicated and conscientious officer finally exacted a heavy toll from Bose. Records show that he was often on tour with least regard to his health. In 1911-12 he spent 114 days on tour and in 1913-14 he was out of the headquarters for 120 days on official duty. In 1923 and 1924 he had to avail of medical leave owing to failing health for almost 14 months.[54] After a most eventful career spanning over two decades, the welfare-oriented administrator and passionate lover of archaeology finally breathed his last on 26 April 1925,[55] leaving behind him a temporary void in the archaeological study of Mayūrbhañj.

References

1. N. Senapati (ed.), *Orissa District Gazetteers,* Mayurbhanj, (1967), pp. 47-91. There is an elaborate discussion on this in Snigdha Tripathy's *Inscriptions of Orissa*, Vol. VI (1974) 'Introduction'. She has also classified the Bhañjas of Orissa into three groups listing the various sources of their genealogy and history.
2. *Ibid.*, pp. 1-2.
3. *Ibid.*, pp. 47-52.
4. *Ibid.*, pp. 1-2.
5. For detailed list, *see Orissa District Gazetteers*, Mayurbhanj, (1967), pp. 58-60 and R.C. Majumdar (ed.), *The Age of Imperial Kanauj*, (1955), pp. 76-77; S. Tripathy, *Inscriptions of Orissa*, VI, 1974, Bhubaneswar; R.C. Majumdar, *Outline of the History of the Bhanja Kings of Orissa*; *IHQ*, XXVIII, 225 ff.
6. A. Joshi, *History and Culture of Khijjinga Kotta*, (1983), pp. 11-13.
7. N. Senapati (ed.), *Orissa District Gazetteers*, *op.cit.*, pp. 57-58.
8. *ASIR*, XIII, 1874-76, pp. 72-73.

9. A. Joshi, *op.cit.*, pp. 13-14.
10. 'Jainagar Expedition of Sultan Firuz Shah' — Extract of translations from *Siraz-i-Firoz Shahi*, *JASB* (Letters), (1942), p. 59.
11. N.N. Vasu, *ASM* (1911), p. 5.

    A. Stirling, *An Account, Geographical, Statistical and Historical of Orissa Proper, or Cuttack* (Calcutta, 1904), Reprinted in *OHRJ*; R.P. Chanda, *History of Mayurbhanj* (1751-1861) Pt. I (1949), p. 59; D.M. Praharaj, *Tribal Movements and Political History of India* (1988), pp. 21-34.
12. P.K. Mishra, *Political History of Orissa, 1900-1936*, (1979), pp. 85-86.
13. D.M. Praharaj, *Tribal Movements and Political History of India* (1988), pp. 81-83, and N. Senapati, *Orissa District Gazetteers*, *op. cit.* *See* the Report of Bose, pp. 38-42.
14. *The Archaeological Survey of Mayurbhanj*, 1911, Preface, p. III.
15. S.K. Patel, *Cultural History of Early Medieval Orissa* (1991, New Delhi), Chapter I.
16. *Ibid.*, Preface, p. vii.
17. *Ibid.*, Preface, p. vii.
18. D.M. Praharaj, *op.cit.*, pp. 80-81.
19. S.N. Sarkar, *Biography of Maharaja Sriramchandra Bhanj Deo* (1918), p. 131.
20. S.N. Sarkar, *op. cit.*, p. 110.
21. *Ibid.*, p. 111.
22. *Final Report of Panchpir Settlement*, 1908-09 to 1911-12 by D. Bhaduri Settlement Officer, p. 13.
23. Final Report on Panchpir Settlement, *op.cit.*, p. 11.
24. S.N. Sarkar, *op.cit.*, pp. 110-11.
25. *RAM*, 1911-12, p. 9.
26. *Ibid.*, p. 17 and p. 22.
27. *Ibid.*, 1911-12, No. 8, p. 22.
28. *Ibid.*, 1914-15, No. 4 and *ibid.*, 1916-17, p. 56.
29. *Ibid.*, 1916-17, No. 13, p. 34.
30. *Ibid.*, 1921-22, p. 8.
31. P. Acharya, *Studies in Orissan History, Archaeology and Archives* (1969), p. 329.

32. P. Acharya's article 'Monuments of Khiching' published in the *Mayurbhanj Gazette*, October 1934, No. 1.
33. *ASI*, 1922-23, pp. 127-28.
34. P. Acharya, *op.cit.*, (1968), p. 367.
35. *RAM*, 1907-08.
36. *IHQ*, XIII, pp. 427-28.
37. *ASI*, 1922-23, p. 126.
38. *OHRJ*, VIII, p. 139.
39. A. Joshi, *History and Culture of Khijjingakotta*, p. 114.
40. *OHRJ*, XIII, No. 2, pp. 4-5 and A. Joshi, *op.cit.*, p. 31.
41. A. Joshi, *op.cit.*, p. 114.
42. *ASI*, 1923-24, p. 87.
43. *Ibid.* and A. Joshi, *op.cit.*, p. 116.
44. N.K. Sahu, *Buddhism in Orissa* (1958), pp. 212-14.
45. R.P. Mohapatra, *Jaina Monuments in Orissa,* pp. 115-16.
46. *ASI*, 1922-23, p. 127 and 1923-24, p. 87.
47. N.K. Sahu, *Buddhism in Orissa* (1959), p. 214.
48. *Ibid.*
49. A. Joshi, *op.cit.*, p. 152.
50. *JBORS*, IV, pp. 172-77.
51. *IHQ*, XIII, p. 42 ff.
52. Antiquities Register, Baripada Museum, and N.N. Vasu, *Archaeological Survey of Mayurbhanj, see* the list of Illustrations.
53. R.P. Candā, *Bhanja Dynasty of Mayurbhanj and their Ancient Capital, Khiching.*
54. *RAM*, 1923-24.
55. *Ibid.*, 1925-26, p. 100.

2

Archaeology of Haripur

AFTER the death of Mahārājā Śrīramcandra in 1912 during the minority of his eldest son Pūrṇa Candra Bhañj Deo, the state administration was entrusted to the Court of Wards. During 1912-22 the Court of Wards did not evince much interest in archaeological pursuits. Whatever work was done to promote archaeology in Mayūrbhañj was due to the personal efforts of Kāmākṣyā Prasād Bose who had successfully combined his official duties with the study of archaeology and preservation of antiquities. Though his failing health in the early 1920s did not allow him to take an active part to promote archaeological study, he motivated Pūrṇa Candra Bhañj Deo, the newly-crowned Mahārājā (1920-28), to invite Ramā Prasād Candā, an eminent archaeologist and historian to complete the unfinished task of Mahārājā Srīrāmcandra.[1] When R.P. Candā arrived at Baripāḍā, Kāmākṣyā Prasād personally took him round the important sites, notwithstanding his precarious health condition. This showed his love for the state he had faithfully served as a loyal officer.

However, the 1920s proved to be a turning point in archaeological activities. A new era began in the study of the history and culture of the Bhañjas. Noteworthy are the scholarly works of Ramā Prasād Candā and the life-long dedication of Kāmākṣyā Prasād's only son Śailendra Prasād Bose, popularly known as Bīrbal Bābū. The life and career of Bīrbal Bābū had a very close association with the monuments of Mayūrbhañj as the following discussion would reveal.

Śailendra Prasād Bose, born at Dhamrāī (now in Bangladesh) on 12 January

1899 had his early education at Baripāḍā wherefrom he passed the matriculation examination in 1915 securing First Division. In those days Calcutta fascinated young men of Bengāl and Orissā aspiring for University education. Śailendra's father Kāmākṣyā Prasād Bose who was keen on giving the best education to his son got him admitted at the Presidency College, under Calcutta University. Śailendra passed the Intermediate in Arts securing First Division and the B.A. Final. Apart from being a good student he had become quite popular among his friends for his interest in sports, drama and music.[2]

In the early 1920s the upsurge of Indian nationalism had turned Bengāl into a cauldron of political upheaval. The call of Mahātmā Gāndhī to join the Non-Cooperation Movement was quite irresistible for the young generation and the Bengalī elites. Śailendra was baptized in nationalism in the pre-Non-Cooperation movement period and he showed an inclination for ultra nationalism for which Dacca and the adjacent areas were famous. He also participated in the Non-Cooperation Movement as a true nationalist. But the abrupt suspension of the movement in early 1921 was a frustrating experience for him. The prevailing situation coupled with the failing health of his father prompted him to return to Mayūrbhañj. The young Mahārājā Pūrṇacandra Bhañj Deo's personal liking for him resulted in his appointment in the Domestic Department in 1924. Śailendra loved music and played the harmonium well. This artistic attribute brought him closer to Pratāp Candra Bhañj Deo, the younger brother of the Mahārājā and later forged a very warm relationship between them. His close association with the members of the royal family also resulted in a temporary assignment as the Private Secretary to the Queen of Bastar state. But his sojourn at Jagdalpur did not last long and the illness of his father finally brought him back to Baripāḍā. After the passing away of Kāmākṣyā Prasād in 1926 the Mahārājā appointed Śailendra as Supervisor in the Department of Archaeology on 1 April 1927. This appointment appears to be providential as the future events would show. Nobody knows what credentials Ṣailendra Prasād had possessed to deserve this appointment; but his career and activities more than any formal qualification vindicated his claim to such an honour. He could prove a worthy son to his worthy father who was the founder of archaeology in Mayūrbhañj.[3]

In his capacity as Archaeological Supervisor Śailendra Prasād Bose had to work with Paramānand Ācārya, the State Archaeologist. Ācārya was trained in archaeology by Ramā Prasād Candā who during 1922-23 to 1928-29[4] had worked as the honorary advisor in archaeology in the State. R.P. Candā of the Archaeological Survey of India and R.D. Banerjee, Professor of Ancient Indian History, Benares Hindu University wrote several authentic books on Orissan History. Candā compiled *History of Mayurbhanj* (Calcutta, 1949) and *Selections from Official Letters and Records Relating to the History of Mayurbhanj*, Vol. I and II (From 1761-1767) (Baripāḍā, 1942). R.D. Banerjee highlighted the history of the Bhañjas in his work *History of Orissa*, 2 vols. (Calcutta, 1930-31) which remained a pioneering work in Orissan historiography. The State had taken steps to have trained persons for the Department of Archaeology. Ācārya had been to various places in India and to London to receive necessary training in Pre-historic archaeology. He was very often on tour outside the state. Therefore the appointment of Śailendra Prasād proved helpful to promote archaeological research in Mayūrbhañj. He visited famous sites in Mayūrbhañj like Haripurgarh, Pratāppur, Baidipur, Bādśāhī, Podadiha, Udala, Kaptipada, Nāranpur, Kuṭing and Pathuriāgarh to gain first-hand knowledge about their historical importance. He also visited Khicing to further explore the potentialities of excavated sites like Virāṭgarh, Itāmuṇḍiā, Chaulkunji, Kīcakgarh, Ṭhakurānīsal, Śaṅkuā Rājār Garh, Dedhsurā Bhāibāhu Temple, Kukudagarh, Sukuruli, Pārvatīpur, Pansī, Ulaykundi, Ghāgī, and Khaṇḍiadoro to chalk out a plan for the future. The interest of the Mahārājā to preserve the rich antiquities of Khicing was translated into reality when J.A. Page, Superintendent of Archaeological Survey of India, Central Circle furnished a plan for a Site Museum at Khicing. The construction of the museum building was completed under the supervision of Śailendra Prasād in 1928.[5]

The sudden death of Mahārāja Pūrṇacandra Bhañj Deo on 21 April 1928 was a severe jolt for the state administration. He was an enlightened ruler who had made determined efforts to improve the affairs of the state. He was succeeded by his younger brother Pratāp Candra Bhañj Deo who was equally enterprising and progressive in outlook. The first archaeological work he accorded approval to was the excavation of Haripurgarh, a medieval township and former capital of Mayūrbhañj. In the absence of Paramānand Ācārya, the State Archaeologist who was away in Calcutta to work with R.P. Candā during 1929-30, the excavation work at Haripurgarh was entrusted to Śailendra Prasād Bose[6] as the Supervisor of Archaeology.

Haripurgarh

In 1906 Nagendra Nāth Vasu had visited the ruins of Haripurgarh, situated about 15 km from Baripāḍā on the right bank of Budābalaṅga river. His study of the history had revealed that the Bhañjas ruled over Mayūrbhañj from Haripurgarh before shifting to Baripāḍā in the eighteenth century. Haripurgarh's earlier name was Hariharpura. The capital city was founded by Mahārājā Harihara Bhañj in 1322 Śaka era, corresponding to AD 1400. It appears that after Khijjiṅgakoṭṭā was destroyed by Feroz Śāh Tugluq in 1360-61, the Bhañja capital was transferred to Hariharpura. For almost 400 years the place served as the administrative headquarters of Mayūrbhañj. The place was strategically located and the area being fertile and prosperous could sustain an urban population. Not far away from the township was the fort of Kusumiā or Banakaṭigarh which must have been used for defensive purposes by the rulers on special occasions.

Hariharpura has been referred to in the Gauḍiya Vaiṣṇavite literature since Śrīcaitanya had passed through this place on his way to Purī in the early part of the sixteenth century. The *Kadaca* of Govinda Dāsa has made copious references to this fact. He writes :

> Next day we reached Suvarnarekha and were glad to see Raghunatha Dasa there. We started thence for Hariharpura where Nemai (Śricaitanya) chanted the name of Hari in ecstasy, and while dancing became unconscious and fell on the ground.[7]

The road from Bengāl to Purī passed through Hariharpura. In a Muslim chronicler's account, there is a reference to the place.

Badaoni writes :

> The Bengal king (Sulaiman Karrani) despatched a force under Kalāpāhār, his general, to Orissa across Mayurbhanja and thence southward by the Kāsābāsā river. Kalāpāhār ravaged Orissa, defeated the Raja's Deputy and shortly afterwards the Raja himself was killed and the Muhammadans finally conquered Orissa in 1568 AD.[8]

Since the invasion of Kalāpāhār in 1568 depredations on Mayūrbhañj became more frequent. This compelled the Bhañja kings to seek shelter elsewhere. Daud Khān, the ruler of Gauḍa had taken refuge in Hariharpura to escape the invasion of Emperor Akbar. From *Akbarnāmāḥ* it is known that Daud took refuge in the Hariharpura fort on 3 March 1575.[9] At that time Baidyanāth Bhañja was the Rājā of Mayūrbhañj. So far the Bhañja rulers were the followers of Śāktism. But in the later part of the sixteenth century Vaiṣṇavism was propagated by Rasikananda, a prominent desciple of Srīcaitanya in Mayūrbhañj. He met Baidyanāth Bhañja at Rājagaḍa near Hariharpura, because the Rājā's palace was under the occupation of Daud Khān. Baidyanāth Bhañja along with his two brothers received Rasikananda and accepted the gospel of Śricaitanya preached by the Vaiṣṇavite Saint. Rasikānanda became their spiritual guide and the Bhañjas thereafter started espousing the cause of *bhakti* cult. As a mark of profound respect for his *guru*,. Baidyanāth Bhañja constructed the beautiful monument of Rasikarāya at Hariharapura. The temple was made of burnt bricks in Gauḍiya style with decorative designs on the outer surface. It was a unique shrine built by the Bhañja king as the architecture of the temple had no parallel in Orissā. Baidyanāth Bhañja was also the builder of the famous Jagannāth temple at Baripāḍā. His successor Jagateśvara was also a follower of Gauḍīya Vaiṣṇavism. During the century that followed the death of Baidyanāth Bhañja, a few more Vaiṣṇavite shrines were erected in and around the capital. These were: Rādhāmohan and Lakṣmī-Nārāyaṇa temples at Hariharpur and the Guṇḍica temple at Vṛndābanpur Śāsana, adjacent to it. In the reign of Rājā Bīra Vikramāditya the Telaṅga gate of Hariharpura was decorated and surmounted with *cauri*.

The reign of Alivardī Khān, the Nawāb of Bengāl (he died in 1754) was one of constant threats of invasion against Mayūrbhañj. Alivardī behaved with great cruelty against the people of Mayurbhañj and their Rājā. The country side was plundered and innocent people put to death. This compelled the Rājā to transfer his capital from Hariharpura. The ruthless depredations of the Marāṭhā army to exact *cauth* from the Rājā was also responsible for the transfer of capital. It was Rājā Dāmodara Bhañja (1761-1796) who escaped from Haripurgarh in the guise of a recluse. The city was devastated by the Marāṭhās. They destroyed the fine and picturesque palace of Hariharpura and the city became desolate. They did not even spare the temples and shrines. What was once upon a time a prosperous township studded with beautiful monuments and palaces lost its splendour for ever and was turned into ruins. This happened some time in 1791-92.

The depredations of the Marāṭhās continued in the time of Rānī Sumitrā Bhañja (1796-1811) till the advent of the East Indian Company in 1803. To protect the images of Rasikarāya and Rādhāmohana, the royal family had shifted them elsewhere. But the image of Lakṣmī Nārāyaṇa could not be saved. The Marāṭhās took the fine image to Bālāsore and left it there. Rānī Sumitrā granted some land for the worship of the deity at Remunā. Though government records mention Hariharpura *kilā* as the abode of the Rānī, she was actually not operating from there. Baripāḍā was the new seat of Government.

A century later in 1906 when Nagendra Nāth Vasu visited Hariharpura (called Haripur), he found the city in complete ruins. He observed the eastern side of the fort measuring 1091', western side 1102', northern side 652' and southern side 686'. On the southeast corner of this area stood the beautiful temple of Rasikarāya covered with trees. The brick temple had still retained some of its decorative embellishments and representations of stories from Hindu mythology notwithstanding its damaged condition. This was a rare brick temple of Gauḍiya style having no match in artistic excellence elsewhere in Orissā.

Of the other ruined structures, Vasu noticed the vestiges of the Queen's abode to the north of the courtyard of Rasikarāya temple. The structure consisted of the seraglio and the bath-rooms. There was no evidence of the living apartments, though the debris was a huge heap of ruins. The *darbār* hall once stood to the east of the debris and north of the Rasikarāya temple. Vasu could unearth a portion of the floor and decorated wall covered with plaster works. He excavated only a small space of the spacious palace and failed to form an idea about the real size and nature of the royal residence.

The Rādhāmohan temple stood to the north-west of the palace. It is a plain rectangular structure made of bricks and plastered with lime. Its architecture was designed in such a way as to separate the sanctuary from the outer hall by a perpendicular wall. Its workmanship is inferior to that of the Rasikarāya temple. The paintings on the wall of the *Naṭamandira* represented Hindu deities, but they were defaced. However, inside the niches the pictures of Vāmaṇa, Matsya, and Jagannāth, etc. were still there. The builder of the temple was Rājā Vīra Vikramāditya Bhañja.

Another temple seen by Vasu was of Jagannāth at a distance of 270' to the south-west of the Rasikarāya temple standing outside the fort area. The original image of Jagannāth was shifted to the nearby village, Pratāppur. According to local tradition the builder of this temple was Harihar Bhañja, the founder of the capital city. This temple too represented Gauḍīya tradition and was decorated with paintings in beautiful colours.

The opposite structure, known as the Rasikarāya temple is conspicuous for its fine workmanship on the outer surface. Architecturally this temple bears resemblance with the temple of Viṣṇupur in Bengāl constructed by Rājā Vīra Hambīra and his descendants. It is a specimen of Gauḍa architecture built by architects from Bengāl. The temple consists of two parts, the main temple and the *Naṭamandira*. N.N. Vasu found the *Naṭamandira* in total dilapidation except for one or two brick pillars representing the lost grandeur. The *Naṭamandira* portion is 49 long and 23' broad. The size of the main temple is 30 long, 27 '6" broad. The *sanctum-sanctorum* which contained the idol appears to be very small. The walls around north, south and east are 3 4" in thickness, whereas in the west the wall's thickness is 7 '. This fine monument although in ruins could be saved at the last moment to represent Gauḍīya Vaiṣṇavism (Neo-Vaiṣṇavism) as it prevailed under the patronage of the Bhañjas. The deula with the curvilinear roof crowned by a bent dome does not conform to the design of a typical Orissan temple. Its main entrance is in the west, though there are openings on all four sides. The main entrance has an excellent ornate frame measuring 12' 9" across with four major bands on each sides of the door. Most of the decorative portions are in damaged condition. The facade in front of the entrance is the most decorative part of the shrine. At the base of the facade can be seen battle scenes at the bottom and amorous scenes of Kṛṣṇa at the top. Some of the decorative panels have been preserved at the Baripādā Museum. The interior surface of the temple was originally covered with frescoes.[10]

Apart from the above-mentioned monuments from the ruins of Haripur an image of Mahiṣasurmardinī of great artistic value had been recovered. Another image discovered there represented Koṭasinī or Koṭavāsinī, which N.N. Vasu presumed to be the presiding deity of the fort. He observed traces of Tāntric Buddhism in the iconogaphical features of this image.

The observation of N.N. Vasu being very superficial, the State Government in 1929 decided to undertake a thorough excavation of Haripurgarh and to preserve it for the posterity after conservation of the structures. Accordingly Śailendra Prasād was assigned with the work of excavation. He worked there during the summer season of 1929 and also in July-August along with the State Engineer. At the initial stage he had complained about the inadequacy of the sum allotted by the authorities for doing the work. He wrote to the Senior Archaeological Scholar (P. Ācārya):

> I am afraid the amount sanctioned would be quite insufficient for even nominal work of conservation.

He had been given an advance of Rs. 250 to start the work. After spending the amount he asked for a fresh advance of Rs. 250.[11] From a report prepared by him on 8 August 1929 we come to know that during the visit of N.N. Vasu the place was fully covered with jungles. N.N. Vasu's excavation work instead of carefully exposing the structures had actually disturbed the site. The Report further says that a renovation of the Rasikarāya temple could have been possible in 1906 and that would have saved the monument with much of its decorated surface and pillars which had supported the roof of the Jagamohana. Thereafter Śailendra Prasād writes about the work done by him as an archaeologist.[12] He writes :

> I found the place completely hidden by thick grown bushes and trees. The top of the temple of Rasik Roy was not visible owing to dead roots and thickly grown Bar (Banyan tree) and other trees. No trace of the *Natamandir,* and the raised platform 13' in breadth all round the temple and the *Natamandira* could be seen before I cleared the area and did some excavation.

The preliminary steps taken for conserving this temple consists of the following works done by me with the sanctioned amount of Rs. 500.

(a) The site to the distance of 50' round the temple and the *Naṭamandira* has been cleared by digging out all the roots of both dead and living trees.

(b) The debris and the earth to a depth varying from 7' to 1'6" have been removed and this has exposed the constructions which were buried and hitherto unknown.

(c) The top of the temple has been cleared by removing the loose concretes, dead roots and living trees.

(d) The top dome half of which existed, above the central dome of the temple and which was in a most unsafe condition has been secured by removing the network of roots and by setting bricks in their original position with strongly prepared mortars of sand and lime. A support wall has also been supplied to the broken arch.

(e) The joints of the walls and the arched domes which were full of earth and broken bricks were dug out to a depth of 2 'and cracks of dangerous type were visible after a considerable clearance. These defects were thoroughly and carefully constructed with bricks and mortar and also by filling in the cracks by forced grouting.

(f) A temporary fencing has been put all round the cleared site, which covers an area of nearly 2 acres.

(g) The ground all round the temple and the *Naṭamandira* has been levelled so that rain water may not stand in the vicinity to damage the constructions.

(h) Niches inside the sanctuary have been repaired and some deeply dug holes in the eastern wall by some unknown persons in search of hidden treasure, have been filled in by bricks and mortar.

(i) The western support wall of the topmost dome, which was out of plumb with a bulged out middle and had a big crack in the centre running from the top to the bottom of the temple, has been strongly repaired by resetting the bricks. The western portion of this dome went down long ago. This dome was originally constructed after filling in the gap beneath with sand.

A few roots of trees and creepers could not be removed now. Because if they will be handled now the whole roof may collapse. When the roof will be repaired they will have to be removed slowly by taking out the bricks and after clearing the roots from that position, the bricks should be reset in their original positions with new mortar.

At present the temple is secured against immediate collapse. But it is necessary at an early date to repair thoroughly the roof and the cracks which run vertically from the top to the bottom. A strong fencing either pucca or of galvanised wire is necessary to secure against the robbing of the decorative bricks set on the pillars and the 4 corners of the temple. It is beyond possibility to repair the *Naṭamandir*. The repair of the roof of the temple and the construction of the Jagamohana will cost a considerable amount, as it will involve massive construction.

Śailendra Prasād's concern for the conservation of the monuments prompted him to prepare a site plan showing the location of the structures and suggesting a future course of action. He prepared and furnished detailed measurements of the Rasikarāya temple and the decorations embellished on it. There were terracotta decorations and curved bricks whose safety in future was a genuine cause of worry to him.

He conducted a survey of the fort area. There were several rooms in the palace and a garden in front with flower beds of geometrical pattern. The palace area measured 1200' x 850' and there were three big wells and two tanks inside. All the structures were of burnt bricks. In the habitation area Bose brought to light the existence of houses in two definite layers showing clearly that the upper one was built on the ruins of the lower one. It was not possible to ascertain the reason of abandoning the earlier settlement and the date of construction of the later habitation. He found the drainage system of the early constructions highly perplexing because earthen pipes were found inserted in the middle of the walls. In the early part of 1930 he took up the conservation work of the southern part of the excavated area of the palace and the walls of the rooms were reconstructed with bricks up to a uniform height with mud mortar. He got the *abhiṣeka maṇḍapa* (consecration *pandal*) repaired with lime mortar, giving an impression of the original technique. A few flower beds were also repaired with lime mortar. Some portions of the southern and eastern side of the palace were excavated from the ground level which brought to light three underground chambers full of debris. In the south-west corner a well was found out. During excavation several broken utensils of metal and china clay, canon balls, bullets, etc. were found. The discovery of the few coloured porcelain utensils and broken dolls was quite interesting. Some terracotta images showed excellent workmanship. The stone sculptures unearthed from the site were also of high artistic value.[13] Regarding the cause of desertion of the fort Śailendra Prasād writes,

> From the way in which all the antiquities were found scattered and from the seign of ash and charcoal everywhere it seems that the palace was barbarously burnt down and all articles were looted and destroyed.[14]

In those days roads and communication facilities in the state were neither adequate nor modernised. Śailendra Prasād had to commute daily on bicycle to the excavation site. The unsafe jungle road infested by wild beasts, however, did not prevent him from discharging his duties sincerely.[15] By hard labour and deep love for historical studies he could complete the conservation work at Haripur to preserve for the posterity a very important piece of monument built by the Bhañja rulers. Whatever suggestions he had made on the line of conservation of Haripurgarh had received approval. The permission to construct a lime kiln for supplying mortar during conservation work was granted on 22 May 1929.[16] He spared time to prepare a detailed report of the work done by him at Haripur.[17] The monuments of Haripur besides exhibiting a new aspect of the religious proclivities of the Bhañjas also bear proof of the spread of architectural tradition of Bengāl into Orissā when the temple building activities of the Bhubaneśvar School had ceased to be operative. The archaeological works at Haripur gave Śailendra Prasād valuable experience to shine in future as a very promising archaeologist and conservator of monuments. His deep interest in archaeology and conservation work created a very good impression in the mind of the Mahārājā who deputed him to Calcutta for special training.[18] He stayed in Calcutta from 21 September 1929 to 20 January 1930, working under the direct supervision of Paṇḍit T. Gāngooly. At that time P. Ācārya who was working in various Record Rooms at Sambalpur, Midnāpore and Calcutta, etc. wanted the services of Bose to collect historical data relevant to Mayurbhañj. Ācārya was in need of a Bengālī scholar to go through the Bengālī Manuscript records. But Gānguly did not spare Bose, for which Ācārya complained to the Mahārājā that a valuable opportunity was lost. Ācārya's letter to the Mahārājā dated 13 January 1930 states :

> In this work I required the assistance of Babus A.K. Mitra and S.P. Bose. Babu A.K. Mitra has been asked to assist me, but Babu S.P. Bose was not spared by Pandit Gangooly. I am sorry to say that Babu S.P. Bose, an officer of the Archaeological Department, had to loose another opportunity in acquiring practical training.[19]

Bose was an avid reader of the original sources of the Muslim period of Indian history to study in-depth the events leading to the fall of independent kingdoms. In this context he read *Riyaz-us-Salatin* and *Tabaquat-i-Nasiri*. That his services were found to be indispensable to the State Department of Archaeology from the beginning was clear from a letter of request made by P. Ācārya to the Mahārājā. Even after Bose was transferred to Khicing on a special work, Ācārya requested the Mahārājā to allow Bose to work at Haripur in addition to the assignments given to him at Khicing. He got the approval of the Mahārāja for the following programme involving Bose at both the sites.

Programme of work of the Archaeological Department for the year 1930-31

1.	April to June	Conservation at Haripur by Babu S.P. Basu and the clerk.
2.	July to October	Conservation at Haripur by Babu S.P. Basu and the clerk. Record work by Babu P. Acharya.
3.	November to December and part of Jan. 1931	Works at Khicing by Babu P. Acharya and S.P. Basu and the clerk.
4.	Part of January to March 1931	Works at Khicing by Babu S.P. Basu and the Caretaker. He will have to come to Haripur after the completion of the work there. Excavation at Haripur by Babu P. Acharya and the clerk.

Approved by the Maharaja

Signature
20.3.30.

Sd/-
P. Acharya
Sr. Arch. Scholar
19.3.30

(File 'D' 1930-31 Dt. 20.3.1930 (16).

Therefore, Bose had to work simultaneously at Haripur and Khicing for some time. However, at Khicing, new challenges were awaiting his arrival in 1930.

The vigilance of Śailendra Prasād resulted in the discovery of numerous antiquities from the villages adjacent to Haripurgarh. He conducted trial excavations at the pre-historic sites of Baidipur, Jadipāl, Khanuā, and Dukura, etc. where he found several stone tools of the Neolithic period. He preserved some beautiful specimens for exhibition in the Museum. He maintained very good relations with his senior colleagues and other workers while in the camp and never bothered about personal comforts. Soon after the first phase of work at Haripur was completed he applied to the Mahārājā for privilege leave to go to Dacca to bring his wife and children to Baripāḍā. Those who had worked with him always admired his meticulous care and diligence in performing the responsible duties of a true archaeologist.[20] For such a person, the future was undoubtedly full of promise.

References

1. P. Acharya, *Studies in Orissan History Archaeology and Archives* (1969), p. 329.
2. Information collected from Mamata Bose.
3. Facts collected from Mamata Bose and also *RAM*, 1927-28.
4. *RAM*, 1927-28, pp. 29-30.
5. *Ibid.*, p. 104 and (1928-29), p. 109.
6. *Ibid.*, 1929-30, p. 112.
7. N.N. Vasu, *Archaeological Survey of Mayurbhanj*, p. 7.
8. Quoted by N.N. Vasu, p. 8.
9. H. Blochmann (tr.), *Ain-i-Akbari*, vol. I, p. 375. (as quoted by N.N. Vasu, p. 8).
10. T.E. Donaldson, *Hindu Temple Art of Orissa*, II, (1986), pp. 740-41.
11. S.P. Bose to Senior Archaeological Scholar, Letter dated 30.5.1929.
12. *Ibid.*
13. File 'F', 1929-30, 22 May 1929, pp. 3-7.
14. Report, *op.cit.*
15. File A(1) 1927-28, 1-7-1927 2(21) pp. 1-8.

16. File A, 1930-31, 2 July 1930, p. 4.
17. File 29 and 30, p. 4 containing Tour Diary of S.P. Bose.
18. *RAM*, 1929-30, pp. 3-7 and File 'F' 1929-30, dt. 19.2.1930.
19. File 'D' 1930, Z(14).
20. File 'F' 1929-30, 25 May 1929, pp. 3-7 and *Ibid.*, 19 February 1930; File 'A' 1930-31, 2 July 1930, p. 2; *Also RAM*, 1929-30, pp. 109-12.

3

Archaeology of Khicing

ORISSĀ is a land of temples. From the sixth century to the thirteenth century AD numerous temples were built by the patrons of Brāhmaṇism for the gods and goddesses of various cults. These temples are distributed in the centres of *pañcopāsanā* like Bhubaneśvar, Jaipur, Purī, Koṇārka, valleys of Prācī, Mahānadī, Brāhmaṇī, Rānīpur-Jharial and Khicing. The earliest temples can be seen at Bhubaneśvar represented by the Śatrughneśvara group of temples built in the Sailodbhava period (6th to 8th century). The tradition of building temples in India at first originated in the time of the Imperial Guptas and then spread to other parts of north India. The north Indian tradition and style being present in the temple architecture of Orissā, it is grouped under the Indo-Āryan style. According to the *śilpa* texts the Indian temples are divided into three main groups on the basis of their characteristic features. These are : *nāgara, vessara* and *drāvida*. Their distribution is regional. The *nāgara* style is seen in north India, *vessara* in the Deccan and *drāviḍa* in south India. In the *nāgara* type of temples (also called Indo-Āryan type) one finds the main temple called *vimāna* having a curvilinear tower. In Orissan temples also the *vimāna* is curvilinear in design which gradually ascending upward is crowned by a huge *āmalaka śilā* at the top. The large number of Orissan temples and their varieties have prompted scholars to treat them as a special class called the Kaliṅga style.

The Kaliṅga style of temples were built as per the *Śilpa Śāstra*s of Orissā viz. *Bhuvana Pradīpa, Śilpa Prakāśa*, *Śilparatna Kośa, Baya Cakadā,* etc. In these texts the temple is compared with *puruṣa* or Divine Being and the main parts of a temple from bottom to top are named as *khura, pāda, bada, gaṇḍī* and *mastaka*. There are various other nomenclatures relating to the parts of the temple.[1] Apart from this we find various types of temple architecture in Orissā. For example, the *vimāna* containing the *sanctum sanctorum* and having the curvilinear tower is called *rekhā deula* and the porch in front of it as an adjunct is designated as *pidha* or *bhadra*. The *bhadra* is distinguished by its pyramidal roof crowned by an *āmalaka* at the top. The temples in Orissā generally consist of two structures, the *vimāna* and the *jagamohana*. The *vimāna* and the *jagamohana* or porch are built in the style of *rekhā* and *pidha* respectively.[2] Together they represent a typical Orissan temple. But there are many variations due to the process of architectural evolution. The early group of temples were made of single structure, i.e., *vimāna* and the *jagamohana* was added subsequently in the second stage of evolution. In the third stage (Brahmeśvara, Liṅgarāj at Bhubaneśvar and Jagannāth temple at Purī) three adjoining structures came up along with the *vimāna* in one axial pattern. These new adjuncts, named as *jagamohana*, *naṭamandira* and *bhogamaṇḍapa*, were pyramidal in pattern having *pidha* roof. But at the final stage of evolution as represented by the Sun temple at Koṇārka, the architect deviated from the tradition by separating the *vimāna* and *jagamohana* from the *naṭamandira* / *bhogamaṇḍapa*.[3]

The architects of Orissā had conducted experiments with several other types of temple design too either to conform to the specific instructions of the canons or owing to the influenc of some exotic tradition. This is evident in the Vaitāl temple at Bhubaneśvar which bears the influence of south Indian *gopuram* design. The Rājarāni temple of Bhubaneśvar is yet another example of deviation/ new experiment.[4] For the *Yoginī* cult the canons prescribed the hypaethral design or circular temples having no superstructure. Such temples are seen at Hīrāpur near Bhubaneśvar and Rānīpur-Jharial in western Orissā.[5] In the Central Mahānadī Valley at Bauḍ one comes across the star-shaped or stellate temples which represent a new stylistic variety.[6] Thus, Orissan temples present varieties, justifying their grouping together as a subclass bearing the nomenclature — Kaliṅga style — under the Indo-Āryan category.

Now referring to Khicing we are reminded of the report made by Lieutenant Tickell after his visit to the spot in 1838-39 (*supra*). As an eyewitness he had seen "two temples as part of a circle of sixty similar ones which with sixty corresponding tanks, are placed two miles apart in a circle of 40 miles in diametre." J.D. Beglar in 1874 and 1876 reported about "pillared hall, Vaishnavic and Saivic temples, Buddhist mound, bricks of 12" x 9" x 3", life-size figures, a hut with images", etc. In 1911 the publication of N.N. Vasu's exploration report in Mayūrbhañj appeared without a report on Khicing but which he proposed to do in the second volume that never saw the light of day.[7] In 1922-23 R.P. Candā published a report in the Archaeological Survey of India after visiting Khicing and other parts of Mayurbhañj. His remark "Khicing far surpasses all these sites in antiquity and inportance" was thought-provoking. His report mentioned about the remains of two fortified palaces (known as Virāṭgarh and Kīcakgarh), and remains of sculptures and temples in the Ṭhakurānī's compound. He was eyewitness to "a small plain brick built shrine on a mound of the old temple in the centre of the Ṭhakurānī's compound in which was enshrined the goddess Khijjiṅgeśvarī or Cāmundā whom the modern Bhañja rulers had revered as their tutelary deity. Near the shrine of Khijjiṅgeśvarī he saw the Khaṇḍiā *deula* or the unfinished temple with four walls of the square cella and nothing more. The reason why the temple remained incomplete is not known. If the construction was halted abruptly for some mishap in the royal family there is no record available to support the premise.[8]

Around Khaṇḍiā *deula*, Candā found a large number of sculptures and images lying scattered and some were kept under a shed. He saw in the scattered heap gods and goddesses of all Brāhmaṇical and heterodox sects along with parts of broken temple. Inside the compound were three *Śaiva* temples dedicated to Dhavaleśvara, Jaṭeśvara and Siddheśvara. There was also the temple of Candraśekhara in a dilapidated condition inclining backwards.

About 500 yards from Khaṇḍiā *deula*/Ṭhakurānī's compound was a small temple enshrining Śiva Nīlakaṇṭheśvara. It was in a ruined state and local people referred to it as the Kuṭai Tuṇḍi temple. It was situated very close to the Virāṭgarh and the river Khairbhaṇḍan.

The above-mentioned structures may be assigned to the heydays of Bhañjas of Khijjiṅgakoṭṭā who having suffered setbacks in 1360-61 due to Feroz Śāh Tugluq's invasion were compelled to shift to Hariharpura in AD 1400. All building activities at Khijjiṅgakoṭṭā thereafter ceased for lack of patronage and protection. The non-completion of the Khaṇḍiā *deula* could be attributed to this factor.

The visit of R.P. Candā to Khicing in 1922 along with Kāmākṣyā Prasād Bose (*supra*) held great promise for historical research in Mayūrbhañj. R.P. Candā came to Mayurbhañj at the request of Mahārāja Pūrṇa Candra Bhañj for exploration of sites of archaeological interest. He was sent by Sir John Marshall, the Director General of Archaeology, Government of India. He wrote a detailed report entitled "Bhanja Dynasty of Mayurbhanj and their Ancient Capital."[9] Pandit Tārakeśvar Gāngooly was also with him.[10] The Mahārājā being young and inquisitive encouraged Candā to conduct an excavation. Khicing was considered to be the Rosetta Stone for unfolding the glorious past of the Bhañja dynasty. Candā excavated the Ṭhakurānī's compound. He unearthed the foundations of a few temples including that of Jaṭeśvara Śiva, several pieces of beautiful sculptures which included one of Hara, several Nāga and Nāgin images, and other relics. The Bhañja rulers being Śaivite by faith had held Hara in very high esteem and referred to the God in their copper plate inscriptions. Candā excavated Khicing for another season (1924-25) and proved by dismantling the small brick temple of Khijjiṅgeśvarī that the image was installed on an earthern platform in a temple whose cella measured 35' square at the base. He called it the great temple of Khicing and took it as the abode of the life size image of Śiva.[11] In a subsequent excavation conducted by S.P. Bose in 1934 a small golden Nāga was found from the site whose purpose was probably votive.

R.P. Candā continued to hold the charge of State Department of Archaeology on honorary basis in addition to his duties as the Superintendent, Archaeological Survey of India, Calcutta. P. Ācārya was the Senior Archaeological Scholar and A.K. Mitra, the junior scholar operating from Calcutta. The Mahārājā had evinced interest for an organised conservation work at Khicing. The first work to be done there was the construction of a Museum at the site to preserve and exhibit the antiquities. In order to keep the ancient relics intact and safe it was necessary to arrange the finds in a roofed shed, piece together the broken parts of certain images, place two gates to the shed, raise the ground and supply improved drainage, enclose the entire area with a wall, make further excavations inside and outside the Kiṅcakeśvarī (Khijjiṅgeśvarī) temple compound and the appointment of a permanent caretaker.[12] A sum of Rs. 1800 was provided in the budget for the purpose. This was suggested by J.A. Page, Assistant Superintendent, Archaeological Survey of India, Calcutta and the job was entrusted to Śailendra Prasād Bose for execution.[13] Bose was appointed as an Assistant and posted at Khicing where he stayed for a long period of fifteen years to restore the place to its well-deserved position as an epicentre of Orissan culture.

The site Museum located in a provisional *kaca* shed was in utter neglect prior to the arrival of Bose. There were 87 images and decorative pieces of high artistic value in it. The magnificent door-jambs and lintels of the old temple recovered from the Khaṇḍiā *deula* and set apart to be rebuilt into a new temple of the Goddess Cāmuṇḍā-Khijjiṅgeśvarī was an important exhibit along with the big image of Śiva. S.P. Bose served at Khicing for two terms: (1) 1927-28 and (2) 1930-42. During the first posting his designation was Assistant Archaeological Scholar with P. Ācārya, the State Archaeologist, as his immediate boss. Some of his correspondences reveal that his first posting at Khicing was beset with many problems. He had to shuttle between two places of work (Haripur and Khicing) and at Khicing was not provided with a place to stay or keep his family. The newly-constructed rest shed was temporarily converted to be used as a residence. Bose painfully observed that the SDO at Karañjiā was not very co-operative. He urged upon the State Archaeologist to send small but essential items like measuring tape and iron levellers. With great difficulty he could arrange the stone grinder for making lime mortar. For timber he had to run after the Forest Ranger and for the Museum building plan the PWD overseer had to be frequently coaxed.[14]

The problem of getting labourers in cultivation season was a major hurdle besides the fixing of local daily-wage rates.[15] To arrange bullock carts for carrying bricks was another irritant. His suggestion to engage forced labour (bethi) was turned down by the Sub-Divisional Officer. Notwithstanding all these he was happy to inform Ācārya one-and-a-half months later[16] that the Antiquity godown and cookhouse had been repaired, fencing had been reinforced and a garden in front of the Museum was ready. The climate at Khicing was not very conducive to his health. He was often suffering from fever which forced him to go to Karañjiā for treatment. It was not easy to reach Baripāḍā either. He was thinking of covering the distance from Karañjiā to Bangriposi by foot after recovery. From Bangriposi there was a Light Railway train service to Baripāḍā.[17] On getting information about the discovery of a group of six stone temples in the villages Indpur and Jiuli, he regretted his inability to visit the site immediately on account of ill-health but assured the authorities that he would visit the site soon. His fascination for historical monuments and antiquities was evident in the letter under reference. ("It is very interesting, but for bad health and want of roads to those places I cannot make myself bold enough to visit those places now".)

The completion of the construction of the Museum building at Khicing was followed by thorough administrative work. From a Report on Baripāḍā and Khicing Museum dated 24 February 1936[18] it is known that adequate steps were taken by Bose who was promoted to the rank of Curator of Khicing Museum with effect from 1 April 1935 and posted there permanently on setting up the Museum as per the suggestions of H. Hargreaves of the Lahore Museum.[19] Bose was sanctioned with Temple Construction Allowance and Photograph Allowance for the additional work entrusted to him.[20] The Report stated the following.

(i) A notice board was erected at the gate giving the name of the Museum, the time of its functioning and the rate of admission fee.

(ii) A map of Mayurbhañj State showing location of archaeological sites was displayed.

(iii) All antiquities were numbered and a Stock Register kept ready giving details of antiquities, their places of discovery/recovery and relevant historical information.

(iv) Each exhibit provided with descriptive label as otherwise it was feared that the educational value would be lost.

(v) Coin cabinet and show-cases for other objects like terracotta, Inscriptions, pre-historic tools, etc. were arranged.

These works bear evidence of Bose' sense of responsibility and great care for proper maintenance of the Museum, as a centre of cultural heritage.

It may appear pertinent to mention here that Bose was capable enough to shoulder numerous responsibilities at a time. While holding the post of Curator of Museum at Khicing he could conduct exploration of distant places and collect antiquities. Even later when he was holding charge of Baripāḍā Museum, official orders were issued asking him to conduct archaeological survey work in Sadar and Kaptipada Sub-divisions, adjacent areas at Midnāpore and Bālāsore districts, and Nilgiri state. The order also stipulated :

> He will visit all the important villages in a *parganah* or a *pir* and collect information and write notes on each place bearing archaeological interest. He will go out of the headquarters for at least 20 days in a month from November 1942 to May 1943.[21]

In 1944 when the Kuṭaituṇḍi temple was damaged by severe lightning Bose went over to Khicing for supervising repair work. He was in reality a man of indomitable energy and resolute will and owing to his sincerity of purpose and honesty in public life he succeeded in delivering the results.

At Khicing Śailendra Prasād's activities fell into three main categories : (1) Reconstruction and conservation of temples, (2) excavation of important historical sites; and (3) collection of epigraphs and other antiquities. Apart from the above, he did some notable works of public interest having varied significance.

Reconstruction and Conservation of Temples

The Mahārāja was keen to conserve the monuments of Khicing, for which he launched a special conservation drive from 1931. A small temple enshrining Candraśekhara Śiva was the first monument to be attended to. This *triratha* temple was only 30 high and standing precariously in the Thākurāṇī's compound. Its *amalaka* had fallen but the cella was intact.[22] Since conservation of religious monuments touched a very sensitive nerve of the local people's sentiment, adequate care was taken to do the job with utmost perfection. A few stone workers having expertise on temple art were temporarily brought from Bhubaneśvar. One such artisan was reported to be Bairāgī Mahārāṇā who during his stay at Khicing trained a group of local artisans in the art of stone carving.[23] The temple was carefully dismantled, each stone was serially marked and spread over the compound. Bose personally supervised the work and gained valuable experience. He could reconstruct the temple in a record time of two months.[24] The reconstructed temple though small in size (28 ' high, plinth 1½ ') now stands on the right side of the Great Temple facing east. It has a 6' foundation and 9 ' 4" square base. Its door-jambs and lintel bear beautiful sculptures and the rest of the temple is plain and simple.

The State Government published a short account of the renovation work done for the Candraśekhar temple in October 1931. The account reveals that stones of irregular size and shape had been used for the plinth without any lime mortar or iron clamp. During renovation, ballast and cement concrete of 2 ' thickness was laid for a strong foundation. Instead of undressed stone, dressed stones were subsequently used. A mason from Bhubaneśvar assisted in preparing a few sculptures. Adequate number of iron clamps were provided lengthwise to keep the stones of the outer surface in proper position. The *āmalaka* and *kalaśa* were firmly placed. The ceiling is made of three pieces of stones placed on an corbelled arch. On the top there is a closed chamber. The *śikhara* is sealed by two big stones on which is placed two half cylindrical stones forming the *beki*. The temple is 28 ' high, having 1½ ' *pista* and 6 ' foundation. The cella is 9 '4" square and the door measures 4 ' x 2 '.[25]

From the Ṭhakurānī's compound were discovered the plinths of two more temples. The architectural pieces were carefully preserved in the Museum for display.

Another temple which was reconstructed by the department of Archaeology in 1930-31 was Kuṭaituṇḍi, a Śaivite shrine dedicated to Lord Nīlakaṇṭheśvara.

Though the entire monument was lying buried under earth, some of its architectural pieces containing beautiful sculptures had impressed R.P. Candā profoundly in 1922-25. He had considered the monument as a gem and masterpiece of architecture. In his report it was stated:

> But by far the most precious relic of antiquity at Khiching is the ruined temple of Nilakanthesvara popularly known as Kutai Ṫundi. (In the records of 1925 this temple is referred to as Sarvesvara Siva Temple. *RAM*, 1925-26, p. 99, Para 2). It is a small temple in the Indo-Aryan style without porch. . . . The plinth of the temple is buried in debris. Most of the missing carved stones that decorated the facade of the temple lie buried in the debris that has accumulated around the plinth. When in perfect preservation this temple was really a gem and must have compared favourably with the best of the temples of Bhubaneswar. The spire has a dangerous crack and is sure to collapse unless adequate measures are taken for its preservation. If this masterpiece of architecture is to be handed over to posterity it will probably be necessary to dismantle the whole structure and then rebuild it with the old materials.[26]

After the successful reconstruction of Candraśekhar temple and conservation of Haripurgarh, Śailendra Prasād Bose was a sufficiently experienced person to venture to accomplish similar success with Kuṭaituṇḍi. In the meantime Mahārāja's permission for demolishing the shrine had been obtained and he studied Orissan temple architecture thoroughly on the basis of original texts to become familiar with the characteristics and regional variations. He followed the same technique of dismantling the temple course by course after exposing the structure. The stones were serially numbered and carefully stocked.[27] It was observed during excavation that the temple did not have a strong foundation as only a few layers of stone had gone down to a depth of 5 'below the ground level. The foundation was laid upon a base of 18" thickness made of ballasts, limestone and clay mortar. This weakness had to be remedied before reconstruction. A strong foundation of 8' depth was laid upon a concrete base of 24' x 24' x 2'. Thereafter the old stones were made use of in reconstruction to avoid delay. Apart from using cement as mortar copper dowels and clamps were used to keep the stones in their proper positions.

A thorough search of the nearby tanks, fields and villages were made to trace out the missing stones. Whatever was found was tallied with the architectural and sculptural style of the temple before being restored. The south-east corner front was completely damaged. While restoring the portion, if the original pieces were not available, plain cut stones brought from the nearby quarry at Keśnā (which was probably the original source of chlorite stone) were used for building the temple. Care was taken to ensure the original impact. Elaborate photographs had been taken before the conservation work began for comparison after the work was done. Since P. Ācārya was away visiting Naraj and Bhubaneśvar for a study of Orissan monuments, the work at Khicing was left entirely to Bose. He took one full season during 1931-32 to complete the reconstruction of Kuṭaituṇḍi at a cost of Rs. 3000. A detailed report on the work of conservation and exploration done by him was submitted to the Director General of Archaeology, India.[28] A summary of the Report prepared by S.P. Bose is given here.

The dismantling work began on 24 December 1930 and took one month to be completed. A sum of 275-6-9 Rupees, annas and paise respectively was spent for the purpose. This included the removal of the earth embankment which was put all around the temple from top to bottom (1924-25) to prevent its collapse. For dismantling, the stone pieces were carefully slipped over an inclined surface of the earth embankment, collected carefully and kept in proper position in the open field. The removal work began from the top to proceed downward layer by layer. It was found out that the *pista* was originally a square platform of a single layer of 10" thickness. Above the plinth there were a total number of 29 layers. The foundation consisted of five layers of stones going 5 'below the ground level. The layer below the plinth was of granite and the remaining four layers were made of well-shaped laterite stones. Finally, at the bottom, the foundation of 18" thickness was made of concrete prepared by limestone mixed with clay. But this base was unable to take the heavy load and the temple had subsided 2" from all sides.

Since not a single stone was in its original position and each was found to be damaged by expansion of the oxidised counter sunk iron clamps and iron pegs used as bonding, a drawing of the temple *in situ* was not prepared. After arranging the stones layer by layer on plain ground a key diagram was prepared. Each stone was numbered with zinc oxide paint as per the key diagram to avoid mistakes during reconstruction.

The south-east corner of the temple was so very badly damaged by lightning that the temple was showing a vertical crack from top to the plinth. The north-east corner was intact, but the other two corners did not have half of the stones. There appeared to be a *mukhaśālā*, which could be traced by the existence of two stones *in situ*. This was a decorative projection in the east forming an adjunct to the main temple. However, there was no trace of decoration above the lintel.

During demolition the original *liṅgam* was not disturbed. Since the layers were disturbed a pillar-like base was kept intact for the *liṅgam*. While clearing the sides of the *liṅgam* below the floor level two pieces of gold plates with lotus petal design were found. These gold pieces represented some votive object.

Finally, it was observed that the temple was constructed without mortar and the joints of each stone were so carefully cut that there was no space to hold any mortar in between. The mistake committed by the builders was in putting soft stones of smaller size in the corners of the shrine.[29] Subsequently, certain conservation work at the adjacent site of Itamuṇḍiā and construction of a fence for Kuṭaituṇḍi were done by Bose.[30]

Today Kuṭaituṇḍi in its restored solemnity stands alone on the bank of the Khairbaṇḍan river as a mute reminder to the age of grandeur. The laborious work of restoration has been able to preserve the artistic workmanship of the Khicing school for the posterity. It has a square ground plan and there is no porch in front. It is quite different from the Candraśekhar temple with regard to its artistic embellishment. The Kuṭaituṇḍi temple is highly ornamented on the surface depicting various scenes of religious episodes and mundane activities. There are a number of erotic sculptures too. The entire *śikhara* is embellished with miniature *caitya* arch motifs and as such bears close resemblance with the Mukteśvara temple at Bhubaneśvar. The vertical projections called *pagas* are noticed here in an evolving stage as the corners are not shown as sharp edges. The *pagas* appear like shallow buttresses to suggest an early stage of architectural evolution. As such the temple can be assigned to the early part of eighth century AD. It is crowned not by a trident, but by an *ākāśa liṅga* to denote its cult identity. Though there are three niches on the *rāhapaga* of each facade except the front one, the enshrined *parivāra devatās* have been missing.

For the excellent work of reconstruction and conservation of Kutaitundi temple, full credit goes to S.P. Bose, the Supervisor. The State Archaeologist has bestowed fulsome praise on him in the Inspection note of 1931 and 1932. The notes record —

> Babu S.P. Bose deserves credit for carefully collecting the missing parts of these temples and putting them in their position. His careful search of stones has led to the discovery of a perfectly preserved image of the Sun God from a tank buried under earth.
>
> (*Tour Diary* July 1931).

On a subsequent date he writes —

> Babu Sailendra Prasād Bose deserves thanks for the work.[31]

Again he informs the authorities —

> The reconstruction of the Kutaitundi temple has been carried out with skill and care by the Supervisor Babu S.P. Bose and I must mention that his interest and labour deserve special notice.[32]

The Great Temple

Khicing attracts a large number of pilgrims and visitors everyday for the presiding diety Khijjiṅgeśvarī enshrined in the Great Temple close to the Candraśekhara temple. This temple was not there prior to 1935. R.P. Candā during excavation of the Ṭhakurānī compound in 1922-24 came across the foundation of a great temple which measured 35' square at the base.[33] This foundation represented an old temple's vestiges which had long since disappeared in the limbo of history. The installation of Goddess Khijjiṅgeśvarī on the ruins on an earthen platform was an impromptu affair accomplished at a time when the circumstances were quite unfavourable. Candā observed two things : (i) the old temple had enshrined a lifesize image of Hara with many other lifesize images as *pārśvadevatās* / *parivāradevatās* and *dvārapālas* (now preserved in the Site Museum) and (ii) the temple had collapsed due to weak foundation. It was quite unbearable for the Bhañja ruler, Mahārājā Pūrṇacandra that the family deity was being worshipped in a provisional structure. There was no dearth of materials. Standing on the ruins of the Ṭhakurānī's compound it was quite natural for the king to search for and think of the possible ways and means to restore the monuments besides providing a temple for the family deity. The *Report on the Administration of Mayurbhanj* 1923-24, p. 81 para 5 clearly records :

> Foundations of the original temple in which the God Siva was enshrined have been traced. Over the shrine of the original temple stands a small brick built temple where-in the Goddess Kinchakesvari is at present enshrined. At the request of the people of the locality, the Maharaja (Purnachandra Bhanj Deo) with his brother, the Chhotrai Saheb (Pratap Chandra Bhanj Deo) visited the shrine on the 24th January 1924 and promised to restore the original temple.

In his conservation note J.A. Page, Assistant Superintendent of the Archaeological Survey of India, Central Circle suggested that the brick built shrine of the *Thakurānī* be removed from the compound as its ugliness did not conform to the surroundings. The demolition of the shrine would make construction of a new shrine imperative, he wrote. At the request of the Mahārājā the Director General of Archaeology asked Page to make a plan for a simple structure of Indo-Aryan style. Since it was decided to use the door-jamb, door lintel and three images on the three niches of the old temple in the proposed new temple, the Khaṇḍiyā *deula* (ruined temple) was demolished.[34]

Therefore, the idea to arrange a plan/design was mooted.[35] The weak foundation of the old temple was considered unsuitable for erecting the proposed new structure. The Administrative Report of 1933-34 informs that the Mahārāja was in favour of building a temple of Khicing style.

In 1924-25 the construction of a new temple for Goddess Khijjiṅgeśvarī, the patron goddess of Mayurbhañj, was proposed and accordingly J.A. Page, Assistant Superintendent of Archaeological Survey of India gave a plan of Indo-Āryan style of temple design. As the style of the Khicing temples were different from that of temples of Bhubaneśvar, it was decided by the Mahārājā to have a design of a temple of Khicing style. The plan of J.A. Page was a replica of the Brahmeśvara temple of Bhubaneśvar, the main temple having four subsisiary temples at four corners of the temple premises. He did it so because the old temple of Khicing on which the Goddess was temporarily enshrined was of *pañcāyatana* type — one large temple at the centre having four miniature corner temples. One of the corner temples was *in situ* (the Candraśekhara temple) which was first to be renovated. The design submitted by J.A. Page would have cost the State exchequer several lakhs of rupees. It required some time for taking a decision. J.A. Page received a cash reward of Rs. 3000 for the design he had submitted.

The first thing the Mahārāja did was to build a Site Museum for the better preservation of sculptures for which a large plot of land was acquired to extend the temple compound and fence it with wire.

The non-descript brick temple of the Goddess was demolished and removed from the compound. The Goddess was put in a newly-constructed shed till a proper temple was built.[36]

The matter was delayed for about a few years due to the tragic death of Mahārājā Pūrṇacandra in 1928. It was revived in 1933 when the conservation and excavation works at Khicing were in full swing and S.P. Bose was building the fort there. A letter from the State Archaeologist to the Dewān of Mayūrbhañj dated 1 July 1933 suggested that

> the Supervisor (S.P. Bose) will also prepare a plan of the New Temple similar in design to the existing temples at Khiching for which work he

will have to take measurements of the temples very often to arrive at the proportion of the shrine and *Sikhara* of the new temple to which the old door jambs and lintel are to be fitted.

The above proposal received the Dewān's approval on the same day. This indicates the eagerness of the authorities to go ahead with the project.[37] It is interesting to find that on the same day the Supervisor had submitted a programme of works to the State Archaeologist for approval. The tentative programme for July, August and September 1933 included

1. Conservation of Itamundia and Chandiasal
2. Conservation of the floor of Kutaitundi and other minor works or dressing and polishing
3. Preparation of a Toy temple (model) as desired by the Mahārāja Sāheb
4. Fencing of the site at Kutaitundi.
5. Preparation of the detailed plan and design of the new temple.

It appears that the question of constructing a new temple was in active consideration from 25 April 1933, because on that date S.P. Bose had requisitioned certain articles for the obvious purpose of drawing a temple design. The note indenting the articles goes as follows:

The following drawing instruments are urgently required for the preparation of the detailed plans of the new temple at Khicing and also for the excavation work.

	Name of Instrument	*Approximate cost*
		Rupees/Annas
1.	One Boxwood Foot Rule 4 fold 2', good quality	3.6
2.	Watch shape metal dial magnetic compass with agate cape 2½"	4.8

3.	Mahogany Drawing Board Double Elephant 29" x 42"	30.0
4.	Drawing Pins pattened with handle one Dozen	.1
5.	Round magnifying glass 4"	12.8
6.	Measuring Taper 25' one	3.8
	50' one	4.8
	100' one	6.8
7.	Ivory Protractor and Scale	.1

The above Indent note received Mahārājā's sanction order on 3 May, 1933.

It may appear convincing to suggest that the submission of S.P. Bose' note to the State Archaeologist, the latter's note to the Dewān and approval of the Dewān, all being done on 1 July 1933 were at the behest of the Mahārājā who had given the green signal for the project 'New Temple' two months earlier on 25 April 1933.[38]

It has been mentioned earlier that S.P. Bose was transferred and posted to Khicing as Curator of the Museum with effect from 1 April 1935. The order clearly stated that his posting was "for the construction of the New Temple there". The State Archaeologist took pains to propose that three rooms out of four of the outhouse be converted to a quarters with a compound wall built of mud and a kitchen at an estimated cost of Rs. 60 for the accommodation of Bose and his family.[39]

The design of the new temple took some time to be prepared in 1933-34. It entailed in-depth study of the Orissan canons of temple architecture and observation of the temples of Orissā *in situ*. Bose had to visit Bhubaneśvar and several places in north and south India for the purpose. Finally, he submitted that —

> The new temple will be 64' high with an outside dimension of 24' square. The *garbhagruha* or sanctum of the temple will be 12 'square. The temple will be of 'Triratha' style. A good number of stones from the old temple will be used in the shrine portion (*bāda*) of the temple. Like the existing temple of Khiching the whole structure will be constructed with 'Muguni' granite stone which is available at Keshna and Adipur neighbourhood.[40]

The plan and estimate of Bose finally received the approval of the Mahārāja[41] and budgetary provisions were made. But the Supervisor was holding dual charge of Haripur and Khicing.[42] Despite the heavy workload he developed a profound sense of involvement in the responsibilities entrusted to him. As a deeply religious person he sought the blessings of the Goddess whose shrine he was ordained to build. He thought that the shrine would take 12 years for completion. He searched for a quarry producing fine quality of chlorite and found it at Keśnā. He studied the technique of building an ancient temple by applying his acute power of observation and experience. He visited several temple sites in Orissā and Bengāl to acquire mastery over the craftsmanship. He had a determined will and inimitable self-confidence. Not only he selected proper type of stones but also trained hundreds of local masons in rudiments of geometry, stone cutting and masonry. He drew numerous sketches and diagrams of various parts of the temple and the decorative designs to ensure the quality of production. He was an excellent draftsman and a master artist. All eyes were focused on him. The challenge was a formidable one demanding hard work, dedication, perfect skill, integrity and leadership.

The Annual Administration Report of 1934-35 records with satisfaction that the centre of activities of the department of Archaeology in the year under review was Khicing because of the important work undertaken by it. Before the close of the 1933-34 financial year the work for the new temple had begun. The foundation was excavated in May 1934 and completed in ten days.[43] A sum of Rs. 4000 was sanctioned for collection of materials. To supply chlorite stone the old quarry of Keśnā was reopened. During excavation some iron implements which had been used several centuries ago by the artisans at Khicing were found. At the lowest ground level a foundation of 46 'x 46 'x 13 ' was dug and was covered by several layers of cement concrete. This foundation of five feet concrete made of cement and granite ballast was spread before the advent of the rainy season. The foundation at ground level then measured 43 ' 2" x 43 ' 2" x 12". About 800 blocks of new stone pieces each of 12" thickness were used.[44] To facilitate cartage he improved upon the road conditions between Keśnā and Khicing. A number of persons were engaged as stone cutters, blacksmiths and masons. Bose himself became the master craftsman, learning every art and training his men with the required skill to handle the job efficiently. He was endowed with adequate professional skill and profound self-confidence. There was an occasion of difference of opinion between the Chief Engineer and himself on the technique of levelling which finally ended with the victory of Bose. His sensitive temperament did not allow any professional disputes to go unchallenged. In a desolate place like Khicing he was his own friend, philosopher and guide. The State Archaeologist remained at Baripāḍā and Calcutta most of the time collecting historical records of the British period relevant to Mayūrbhañj. Under the circumstances Bose was doing several things simultaneously. Besides the conservation of Kuṭaituṇḍi he was engaged in the conservation work at Virāṭgarh, Itamuṇḍiā and Chaulkunji, showing complete disregard to his health. The workload was so much that the State Archaeologist used to write from Calcutta expressing personal sympathy.

> I imagine your troubles and hardships in regard to its undertaking. I request you to take particular care of your health although I understand that this advice cannot be adhered to under the circumstances. I still regret that owing to circumstances I was unable to go to Khiching and share some difficulty with you.[45]

After the completion of conservation work at Itamuṇḍiā (Buddhist site) in July 1933 he began focussing on the task of building the Great Temple. He remained busy in final drawing work during July 1933. Though the foundation had been laid he had to pause for a while with regard to the final shape of the proposed *triratha* temple.[46] He requested the State Archaeologist to provide him with a photograph of the Mukteśvara temple of Bhubaneśvar. He was very cautious in proceeding with the Temple project probably because of constraint of funds. In February 1934 he complained about dearth of funds for cartage of cement from

Bādāmpahār to Khicing.[47] The response of the Dewān was very quick of course because he immediately sanctioned Rs. 750.[48] Bose used to draw up a tentative programme for the whole year for obtaining approval of the higher authorities.[49] The work however did not stop and he could complete the foundation 'with great difficulties' by July 1934.[50]

In 1935-36 a sum of Rs. 6000 was provided for the construction of the new temple.[51] The Annual Report reveals that the whole work of laying "8 layers out of 9 of the foundation was done by the masons of the locality who were trained under the direct supervision of S.P. Bose, the Curator of the Khiching Museum."[52] The constraint of funds however, slowed down the progress of work at times.[53]

In January 1935 a revised design of the new temple was submitted to the Mahārājā for approval. The budgetary allocation for 1936-37 was increased to Rs. 8000 for construction of the plinth of the new temple. The work could be accomplished as three layers were laid with cement concrete base and six more were to be added later.[54] This year in April (1935) S.P. Bose was permanently posted at Khicing as Curator of the Museum and was granted special construction allowance and photograph allowance for the nature of job enstrusted to him. The Mahārāja was eager to expedite the work. A sum of Rs. 12,000 was allocated in the year 1937-38 which helped the completion up to the plinth. Even in the rainy season the work did not stop. The Curator trained local artisans to repair and recarve the old stones for use.[55] In 1938-39 the height of the temple could be raised up to 8 '8" above the plinth by using 4500 cft. stone quarried from the mine. A few images from Baripāḍā Museum were removed to Khicing and set on the wall. The state made a provision of Rs. 15,000 in the annual budget. The construction work was done under the direct supervision of S.P. Bose, Curator, Khicing Museum.[56]

The year 1939-40 was an eventful one. It not only saw further increase of allocation but also, the temple was raised to a height of 26 from the ground level. All through the construction no compromise was made with the quality of works. Bose convinced the authorities to purchase steel bars for making pegs and clamps from Calcutta to ensure the use of original articles of high standard. He used to furnish elaborate and convincing reasons for whetever he did[57] and continued to submit his plan of action for the whole year in advance to the authorities.[58]

While constructing the new temple the inquisitive mind of Bose probed into the reasons responsible for the collapse of the original temple. Having found out the reasons, in the Report of his works during 1934-35 to the authorities, he stated :

> It is extremely surprising that inspite of the definite and rigid rules laid down in the Silpa Sastras which emphatically state that the foundation of a temple must be one-third of its total height above the ground level, the builders of this temple provided only one-twelfth of the total height for the depth of the foundation. This neglect of the construction of the foundation is the cause of its early collapse.

He further informs :

> From the scattered available parts I have been able to make out that the temple was a *Pancharatha Rekha* temple almost similar in design to the Muktesvara temple of Bhubaneswar.

His knowledge on Orissan *Śilpa Śāstras* was astounding. Explaining the difference between 'Restoration' and 'Construction', he once wrote to the State Archaeologist:

> The actual work of restoration means the arrangement of the old stones of the great temple in their respective 'Pagas' or pillasters. This work has actually been commenced from July 1937 and now the missing parts are being carved new. The setting of these stones with mortar and in some cases with molten lead will be done when the arrangements of stones will reach the height up to some 20' i.e. upto the end of the vertical portion of the temple. . . .[59]

For the discovery about the defective construction of the Old Temple, Bose was highly commended by the State Archaeologist.[60]

During construction Bose followed the conventional methods to raise huge stone blocks to high altitude for proper placement. The completed part was being progressively buried by earth and a ramp was made with suitable gradient to enable the workers to carry huge blocks of stones to the top of the structure. This was a traditional method of constructing Orissan temples. As it required a large labour force and expenditure, details of the persons engaged in the work with rate of payment to each was maintained meticulously. Even the progress in the work was noted in the form of drawings, diagrams and photographs as evidence on record.[61] His total passion for archaeological work was evident in the above letter in which he wrote :

> I am living with stones, being deprived of society, friendship and love so divinely bestowed upon man.

The State Government was pleased to confirm his services as a Curator with effect from 31 March 1938.[62]

The news of the novel undertaking by the State Department of Archaeology spread far and wide. In January 1939 K.N. Dikṣit, Director General of Archaeology, Government of India paid an official visit to Khicing. He was happy to note the interest the State of Mayūrbhañj had shown in archaeology. The province of Orissā having been created in 1936, it did not have a Department of Archaeology till 1950. Recognising the rich historical potentiality of Mayūrbhañj Dikṣit suggested the appointment of some technical personnel and proper documentation of the pre-historic sites. His Report dated 13 February 1939 mentions :

> Perhaps the most striking piece of Archaeological work done in Mayurbhanj is in the field of conservation and restoration. This is particularly evident at Kutaitundi temple at Khiching which is a fine example of the repair of ancient monuments layer by layer and their restoration is difficult task requiring great care and ingenuity on the part of the supervising staff and it speaks volumes for the efforts of Mr. S.P. Bose that he was able to do this successfully in the case of the Kutaitundi and the Chandrasekhra Temples. It is a matter of satisfaction

> to note that the Maharaja Saheb had now detailed him for the work of restoring the Great Temple in the Thakurani compound where the Tutelary deity of the Bhanja family will be re-installed. Both as regards the knowledge of architecture and literature and its practical application in construction Mr. Bose has acquired sufficient mastery to enable him to accomplish this task. The way in which he is able to determine the exact position of each stone among the thousands lying pell mell in the compound is very creditable. . . . I know of no one in eastern India who has so thoroughly understood the principle underlying the restoration of ancient specimens of architecture and carried them out with such devotion and ability. . . .[63]

Subsequently when the completion of the construction work of the Great Temple was intimated to the Director General of Archaeology in 1941 his response was immediate. He wrote to Ācārya :

> I am glad to hear that at last the great work of the reconstruction of the temple at Khiching has been completed. I am sure it will reflect great credit on all concerned and I must congratulate all of you, particularly Mr. S.P. Bose, on the great knowledge, care and patience brought to bear on this work.[64]

However, the reconstruction of the Great Temple was not an easy task. Apart from the constraints of funds, hindrances caused by natural conditions and problems related to use of roads, there were other factors worrying Bose from time to time. For example, while reconstructing the curvilinear portion of the *Gaṇḍi* he found the expected quantity/number of stone blocs insufficient. By working out the actual requirement he was confronted with a shortage of about 4000 cft. of stone. The problem necessitated provision of funds as well as time.[65] He submitted the budget proposal, for Rs. 6042-14-9 for completion of the work including the removal of earth embankment, finishing touch, cleaning, etc. Along with the proposal, a detailed agenda of work to be done and the cost it would involve was also furnished to the authorities.

Finally, the Great Temple was completed in all respects by the end of 1941 and the deity was installed on 14 March 1942 amidst pomp and ceremony. On the auspicious occasion several ruling princes of Orissā and the entire Bhañja royal family were present along with the Mahārājā. A small inscription in Oriya on the top of the front door recorded that the work of reconstruction was completed in the reign of Mahārāja Pratāp Candra Bhañjdeo by his loyal servant Śailendra Prasād Bose. It was a great achievement in the history of restoration and conservation, a landmark in Indian archaeology. The height of the temple measured 68' above the ground level. A sum of Rs. 80,000 was spent in its reconstruction and conservation.[66] After the work was done, the State Government abolished the post of Curator of Khicing and transferred Bose to the Head Office at Baripāḍā as Curator of Baripāḍā Museum.

Excavation and Exploration

The excavation conducted by Kāmākṣya Prasad Bose in 1905-07 were of a pioneering nature. Though not a trained archaeologist his academic interest motivated him to search for ancient artefacts and objects of art. He, for the first time, had brought to light the hidden treasures of ancient antiquities buried in several sites of Khicing. Except the collection of antiquities and trial digging, not much could be done on account of the transferable nature of his job. The publication of N.N. Vasu's *Archaeological Survey of Mayurbhanj* in 1911 was another encouraging step. But the death of Mahārāja Śrīrāmcandra in 1912 in a sad accident was like a bolt from the blue which placed the State administration under Court of Wards till 1922. All development works remained suspended. In 1922-24 R.P. Candā made the first sincere effort to excavate archaeological sites on scientific lines and published the Report in the Annual Issues of the Archaeological Survey of India. But he too could not reach the goal of a full-scale excavation of numerous sites to unearth the marvels of Khicing. His preoccupation in Calcutta as Superintendent of Archaeology, and efforts to select important letters and documents of the British period to write a complete history of Mayūrbhañj as per the behest of Mahārājā Pūrṇacandra (1922-28) did not allow him a longer tenure at Khicing. The sudden demise oif the Mahārāja (Pūrnacandra

Bnañj Deo in 1928) was also a severe setback to the Rāj family's search for historical identity. A Museum, however, had been set up at Khicing to preserve the precious antiquities collected by Bose and Candā.

During a very short period after his arrival at Khicing, S.P. Bose could collect a number of antiquities from the neighbouring area. His tour diary reveals that from 10 June 1927 to 7 September 1927 he added the following articles to the stock of the Museum:

(i)	10 June	- An image of Nagini from Kichakgarh
(ii)	22 June	- Two broken images of Mahavira from Pandavilla
(iii)	23 June	- One Jaina Tirthankara from the same place
(iv)	30 June	- An oxidised copper implement/object
(v)	9 July	- Three copper coins from Rarua
(vi)	21 July	- Seven old coins from Jashipur
(vii)	22 August	- Some Hindu icons from Jeuli
(viii)	25 August	- Stone Siva Linga from Jeuli
(ix)	1 September	- One Silver Coin
(x)	6 September	- Two Silver Coins with Arabic and Persian legends
(xi)	7 September	- Five Stone Lingam with Sakti, from Jiuli. Six Lingam without Sakti, from Jiuli.

In 1929-30 the transfer of S.P. Bose, Archaeological Supervisor from Haripur to Khicing was motivated by the desire of the new Mahārājā Pratāp Candra (1928-47) to revive archaeological activities there. With the completion of conservation work at Haripur, the Department of Archaeology was in a position to devote full time to such work which held great promise.

The Archaeological Supervisor had in the meantime gathered valuable knowledge and experience in historical archaeology. Khicing was an ideal place for the application of his professional knowledge. To fulfil the desire of the Mahārāja with whom he had very close rapport and to complete the unfinished work of his deceased father were twin responsibilities which he had to discharge satisfactorily. These tasks provided sufficient impetus to his academic inquisitiveness.

Since the main focus of the Mahārāja was on the shrine of Goddess Cāmuṇḍā located in the Ṭhakurānī compound, Bose also supervised the excavation in the compound where a large number of ancient sculptures were buried while demolishing the Candraśekhar Temple layer by layer and keeping key diagrams of each layer. He could find out many missing parts of the old temple and carefully preserved them in the Museum.[67] In an adjacent site called Kukuraghar, excavation work and clearance of debris brought to light the plinth of a stone temple. A small image of Buddha was discovered. The vestiges of the plinth of the temple revealed that it was made of rough grained sandstone. The source of this type of stone could not be ascertained. Bose rightly believed it to be the remains of the Buddhist monument.[68] He was in fact re-excavating the old site cleared by his illustrious father, K.P. Bose about thirty years ago. Another site which the spade of the archaeologist touched brought to light two beautiful images of *Umā-Maheśvara* along with the plinth, curved door-jambs and the decorated lintels of two ruined temples. The local people used to identify the images as part of Dedhasura Bhaibahu temple. A study of the plinth revealed that the structure was of Indo-Āryan variety. Among the two images of Umā-Maheśvara, the big one was enshrined in a temple built of laterite stone, and the smaller one in a brick temple. After clearing vast ruins of stones from the surrounding areas, it was found that the plinth was 15½' square. It had been plastered with mortar. The jambs and the lintel measuring 5½' x 4½' of the big shrine were in a good state of preservation and bore excellent carvings. The standing images of Nandī and Bhairava at the base were carved well. Though the above temple was made of laterite stone, the images of Nāndī and Bhairava at the base were carved with great care and beauty. Though the above temple was made of laterite stone, the images, door jamb, lintel and the finial were of chlorite stone. The *pārśvadevatā*s from the three niches were missing. But a trunk of Gaṇeśa and the lower hand portion of Pārvatī could be found.

The brick temple after excavation showed that the ground plan was similar to that of the Saṅkuā Rājār Garh. It had jambs made of chlorite stone, embellished with beautiful relief work. It is strange that the entrance was to the west.

About one kilometre to the east of the Ṭhakurānī's compound the remains of four brick temples were unearthed at the site known as Chandiāsāl. Among these, two were large and two small. The main temple located at the centre was 12 'x 12 'size at the base, having a 15 'wide verandah on all four sides. The pedestal portion and the upper portion of a Buddha image in earth touching pose was discovered. This discovery provided clue to the identity of the ruined monument as a Buddhist one. Adjacent to the above temple complex existed another building made of brick and stone having a dimension of 46 'x 48 '. It was probably a pillared hall as indicated by the top portion of two broken pillars.

Excavation work was also conducted at Virāṭgarh site situated on the left bank of river Khairbhaṇḍan at a distance of one km from the Ṭhakurānī compound. The surface finds included a vast ruined palace of bricks and habitation area. In 1908 its potentiality had been first realised by K.P. Bose, the SDO of Pañcpīr who had discovered Kuṣāṇa coins, a big earthen jar and a piece of gold from the site. Subsequently, in 1926-27 a stone seal of second century AD had been reported. During the excavation of 1930 the discovery of Kuṣāṇa coins from residential areas provided definite evidence about the period of occupation.[69] Another interesting find from the surface was a stone seal with legend *bhūmi deva* which could be assigned to the tenth century.[70]

In 1931-32 apart from the reconstruction of Candraśekhar temple and the demolition of Kutaituṇḍi temple, priority was given to the continuation of excavation work at Virāṭgarh. The total residential area at Virāṭgarh was found to be 750 ' x 450 ' or about four acres and the team excavated an area of 54 sq ft lying in the middle of the northern side of the river. Here three rooms with verandah were unearthed. The southern room measured 13 '6 " x 13 'with walls measuring 5 ' wide. The height of the damaged/ruined wall was 6 ' or more at places. On the eastern side of the building the size of the verandah was 36 'long and 11 'wide and on the southern end a staircase was observed. Probably, there was an upper storey. At a distance of 9 ' west of the building was found the evidence of a broken wall 3 ' wide.

Among antiquities were found household articles of terracotta, iron and copper. Iron arrowheads, chisels, rods, door nails, mass of lead, molten copper, elephant catching nails along with beads of quartz, stone and glass. Most of these antiquities have found a place at the Site Museum as exhibits.

It was interesting to find that large size bricks were used in construction. The full size bricks measured 16" x 10" x 2" and the half-sized ones were of 9" x 8" x 2" dimension. To join the bricks, mud mortar was used besides occasional use of lime plaster.

Vasulisal was another adjacent site which K.P. Bose had first excavated in 1908, but with no result. But in 1931 S.P. Bose exposed from the site the ruins of the *mukhamaṇḍapa* of a temple of size 11½ 'x 9½ '. There was a platform (*vedi*) to the north of the temple measuring 8 ' x 6½ '.

S.P. Bose spared no pains to execute the excavation work at Karamarājāragarh, a small mound near the Ṭhakurānī's compound. The site was so named because of a Karama tree which the tribal people used to worship during Karama dance festival. There was a Śiva temple in ancient days because in 1908 K.P. Bose had collected the beautiful broken image of *ardhanārīśvara* from the spot. In 1924 the remaining portion was found. After clearance of debris the foundation of a laterite temple of the size of 14 ' x 12 '9" was exposed. There was also another temple of brick surrounded by a compound wall. The temple measured 25 ' x 20 '. The stone and the brick temples were close to each other. To the north of these temples Bose found the ruins of two other small stone temples.[71]

As a result of the above excavations several new sculptures were added to the local museum. Some of the sculptures were sent to the exhibition of the Art of India organised by the Secretary of the Burlington Fine Art Club, London. A small image of Mahisamardinī Durgā similar in style to the image of Marici preserved in Baripāḍā Museum was transferred from Khicing to Baripāḍā. Although the images were iconographically different, their style and technique of art had much in common.[72]

The excavation in 1933-34 conducted by S.P. Bose in a Buddhist site called Itamuṇḍā yielded interesting results. The archaeologist found that on the ruins of a Brāhmanical temple, the Buddhist shrine had been built. There were the images of Kārttikeya and Mahiṣāsuramardinī below the Buddhist shrine. The plinth of the Buddhist monument was raised to a height of about 5' from the ground floor of the earlier building by blocking up the doorways and other openings. The walls were constructed with bricks joined by mud mortar. As very little of the upper structure was traceable, Bose could not compare the materials of the earlier structure with those of the later period. He found, from the ruins, the evidence of three rooms provided with a verandah in the north. The wall was 5' wide and each room had a door leading to the verandah. This could be the remains of a Buddhist monastery. A big image of Buddha occupied the middle room which had a stone doorway. The lintel of the door frame contained the figure of a seated Buddha. It is interesting to note that an image of Mahiṣamardinī was engraved on the right jamb in such a way that it would not be seen directly by the viewers. Further, it may be noted that the image was carved upside down. This suggests that the Buddhist shrine was built with materials collected from the old Śiva temple.

Not far away from the above site in the north Bose found the vestiges of a Buddhist *stūpa*. The excavation of the *stūpa* exposed a small earthen pot containing bones and ashes closed by a lid. Obviously, the object represented some sacred relics being carefully preserved there. Another Buddhist site was Chandiasal situated at a distance of three km from Itamuṇḍiā. Steps were taken for the proper conservation of the area which had been excavated in 1930-31. The ruins represented a brick built structure of a *pañcaratha* temple. Only the *pīṭha* and the first two mouldings of the *pabhaga* had remained intact. The *pada* and *kumbha* were made of beautifully carved bricks. From the ground plan, the ruins revealed clear evidence of a nine-chambered structure of square design each side extending 42'. Bose believed that the structure consisted of four corner rooms of 15' square with the central room of 12' square provided with four verandhas of 15' x 12' each. But in the absence of the superstructure no definite conclusion could be made with regard to the nature of the monument. Adjacent to this was another brick built structure. From the decorative designs on the panels the monument could be assigned to the tenth-eleventh centuries.[73] Though the tradition of building brick monuments was very popular in the Bhauma-Kara period (AD 736-950) it was discontinued later with the building of stone temples. Brick structures were quite popular with the Buddhists who had built the shrines and monasteries at Ratnagiri, Udayagiri and Lalitgiri in the Cuttack district.[74] In the Somavaṁśī period (950-1108) brick was replaced by stone in the coastal districts of Orissā. A survey of the monuments of Upper Mahānadī Valley also reveals that the construction of brick temples (Sirpur, Rājim, Araṅg, Palari and Pujaripāli, etc.) was progressively discontinued in favour of stone temples.[75]

The year under review (1933-34) witnessed intensive and extensive excavation at Virāṭgarh for the third consecutive season. The result was the discovery of at least two distinct layers of habitations one above the other. From the lower stratum were found a large number of household articles, chief among which were copper vessels, stone beads, iron implements and potsherds. These articles had no similarities with the household items discovered from the upper layers. Several Kuṣāṇa and Purī-Kuṣāṇa coins were also found. The discovery of Imperial Kuṣāṇa coins provided clue to the date of Khicing. A study of the Purī-Kuṣāṇa or imitation Kuṣāṇa coins suggests the continuity of Kuṣāṇa rule.[76] In fact the discovery of a large number of Kushana and Purī Kuṣāṇa coins over an extensive region covering the area from Singhbhūm to Ganjam led the numismatists to believe that Orissā was ruled by the Kuṣāṇas and their feudatories for a very long time before the advent of the Imperial Guptas.[77] The large number of Kuṣāṇa and Purī-Kuṣāṇa coins from the Bhañjkiā hoard had led scholars to believe that there was a local mint somewhere in Singhbhum where copper mines exist even today.[78]

The excavation at Virāṭgarh resulted in the discovery of stone and glass of various sizes in large quantities indicating thereby the progress made in bead manufacturing and ceramic industries. The stone beads found in several stages of preparation from natural stone to finished form prove that these were locally manufactured.[79]

Among other interesting discoveries were two small broken seals, one dated to fourth century and the other to the tenth century AD. All these findings furnished clear proof of the historicity of Khicing as a seat of civilization during the early Christian centuries.[80]

The archaeological activities of 1933-34 being very significant attracted the attention of the Mahārāja who paid a visit to the site in June 1933. In February 1934, the Dewān too visited the place and was apprised of the significance of the discoveries. In the Annual Administration Report it was notified :

> The Supervisor deserves credit for conducting the excavation at Biratgarh which was done with due care.[81]

As a result of the royal visit the activities in Khicing received new impetus. To facilitate the construction of the new temple the old chlorite stone quarry of Keśnā was re-excavated. This excavation brought to light some iron implements which had been actually used by the stone cutters in the ancient days. Bose took interest to conduct trial digging at Kīcakgarh where the plinth of a brick structure could be traced. The nearby site of Chaulkunji, famous for the monolithic pillars (four large and ten small) of a huge hall, was protected with green fencing.[82]

For a couple of years the Archaeology Department remained preoccupied with the restoration work of the Great Temple at Khicing. In 1937-38 excavation was conducted at Virāṭgarh, Sukruli, and Deodhipa. At Virāṭgarh a number of potteries were unearthed and drainage was provided to protect the site from damage by the heavy flow of rain water. The excavation of Sukruli brought to light the ground plan of a ruined brick structure which was made of three halls. Its outside dimension was 44 'x 33 '. The hall on the northern side measured 39 ' 6" x 9' 7" and the southern one measured 39' 6" x 7' 9". The walls were 2' 3" in thickness. Quite close to this monument was a mound which after excavation revealed another brick structure. Several antiquities like iron axes, stone pestles, frying sticks, potteries, and beads of quartz, cornelian, and stone were also found.

At Deodhipa the archaeologist unearthed a brick built shrine measuring 14 sq ft. A Śivaliṅga, with the images of bull and Cāmuṇḍa, were collected from the site. There was clear evidence of many temples which had been standing there in the olden days. But the size of the temples being very small their use was probably for votive purposes. Some of the temples were monolithic, made of one stone only. A temple had a *mukhamaṇḍapa* measuring 22 sq ft with a verandah in front measuring 13' 6". Due to constraint of funds further excavation could not be undertaken.[83] In fact the works in old sites slowed in the following year too for financial crunch. Limited excavation in 1938-39 resulted in the discovery of two inscribed terracotta Buddhist *stūpa*s used for votive purposes. Along with the votive *stūpa*s 64 household iron implements were also found.[84]

The archaeological activities of the Curator of Khicing Museum included exploration of the nearby areas in quest of antiquities. He brought to light the existence of a rock inscription of Benusāgar on the border of Mayūrbhañj and Singhbhūm. The Inscription belonged to the eighth-ninth centuries.[85] From the village Ādipur a copper plate inscription of King Durjayabhañja Deva was discovered, along with two other copper plates of King Narendrabhañja Deva.[86]

In 1939-40 two copper-plate grants from Shamsundarpur were brought to light. One of the copper-plates measured 6½" x 5½" and contained a seal representing a lotus flower with 18 petals. The seal was inscribed with the legend *śri raṇabhañja devasya*. From the contents of the grant it was revealed that Raṇabhañja, the donor, was a Mahārāja.

The other copper-plate measured 8.3/8" x 5.3/4". It was in such a damaged condition that except the name of the donor (Durjayabhañja) nothing else could be deciphered. The only copper-plate grant found from the Thakurani's compound on 1 December 1941 was shifted to Baripada Museum for careful preservation. Though the seal is damaged the donor's name is given as Mahada Bhañja Deva.[87]

The most important archaeological finding of the year (1939-40) was the discovery of two hoards of ancient coins near Raruan, not far away from Khicing. A bronze cup containing 105 copper coins of Purī-Kuṣāṇa type was dug out by a worker engaged in road construction. Similarly, from a tank in Bhānupur were found three Gupta gold coins of the time of Candragupta II.[88] These numismatic finds provided new data for the reconstruction of Kuṣāṇa and Gupta rule over Orissā. The authenticity of the Gupta rule was subsequently substantiated by the Sumandala copper-plate of the time of Pr̥thvī-vigraha, dated Gupta era 250 i.e. AD 569-70.[89]

The Director General of Archaeology who paid a visit to Khicing and the excavated sites had expressed satisfaction over the work and the result. He had given detailed instruction as to the way in which accurate and complete records were to be made of the sites, excavated buildings and findings. His observation at Virāṭgarh was very encouraging because in a letter to the State Archaeologist he wrote :

> It is certain that at the Biratgada site at Khiching (as also in other sites such as Kichakagada) lies the key to the more ancient history of Mayūrbhañj and it is, therefore, necessary that further work in this promising field should be undertaken.... From the number of implements of every kind which were apparently buried near the site it appears that the site was abandoned.... From the coins and other finds it appears that the remains at Biratgada can be referred to a date from the fourth to the 5th century AD. When the entire site is excavated it would be possible to understand arrangements of the houses and the town planning. Khiching seems to have an advantage over other town sites in India, in that the remains are comparatively well preserved and they are close to the surface.[90]

The Director General had also suggested steps for the improvement of the Museum at Khicing and Baripāḍā. His main emphasis was on cataloguing the antiquities and issue of publications like *Archaeology in Mayurbhanj* and *Khicing and its Antiquities* for the public to know about the contributions of Mayūrbhañj. The Mahārāja had accepted his suggestion to depute a scholar to be trained by the Archaeological Survey of India in order to strengthen the State Department of Archaeology. Kṛṣṇa Chandra Pāṇigrahī, who had received Post Graduate education in Calcutta University (1935-37) in Ancient Indian History and Culture with stipend from the State Government and had been appointed as a Scholar in Archaeology in 1939, was deputed to the Archaeological Survey of India for intensive training.[91]

After the construction of the Great Temple at Khicing S.P. Bose, the Curator of Khicing Museum, was transferred and posted at Baripāḍā Head Office. During his short tenure he was required to visit a vast area for collection of antiquities and discovery of potential archaeological sites. Touring through the Kaptipada Sub-division, he discovered several images of Hindu and Buddhist pantheon which were brought to the Baripāḍā Museum for preservation and display. A beautiful image of Goddess Cāmuṇḍā seated on *siṁhāsana* and with the conventional attendants was found at Pedagadi. On stylistic considerations, it could be assigned to the eleventh-twelfth century. Another image of Avalokiteśvara found from Puradihi was an excellent specimen of plastic art. The image bore the fineness of artistic work typical of the Khicing school. It was made of fine grained grey chlorite stone. The discovery of one more gold coin of King Candragupta II added great significance to the historical interpretation of the numismatist with regard to the Gupta rule over ancient Orissa.[92]

The State could not sustain its archaeological pursuits with vigour during the period following 1942 when the impact of World War II and the famine in Bengāl was deeply felt. Scarcity of essential commodities had led to the imposition of rigorous control over the distribution system. Public rationing was introduced under the direct supervision of the Mahārāja. The Administration Report in 1944-45 regretfully mentioned that there was practically no work under the head 'Excavation and Conservation' and 'no survey of ancient monuments'. But it was out of dire necessity that the Kuṭaituṇḍi temple damaged by severe lightening on 26 June 1944 had to be repaired. S.P. Bose then stationed at Baripāḍā as the Curator of the Victoria Memorial Museum had to be deputed to Khicing for repairing the damage.[93] Another temple which could not be saved from natural calamity was the temple of Dedhasura-Bhāibāhu at

Khicing. Due to unprecedented rain the flood water of Kantakhair river completely washed away the laterite stone blocks to its bed. Though Bose took pains to recover some of the stone blocks, the temple was lost for ever as no reconstruction was possible.[94]

The Department of Archaeology was headed by P. Ācārya designated as the State Archaeologist. Since he was busy in collecting records from various Archives and Record Rooms, the archaeological work at the Head Office was entrusted to the care of S.P. Bose. It was on the suggestion of the State Archaeologist (P. Ācārya) that Bose was permanently transferred from Khicing to Baripāḍā. In a lengthy note to the Assistant Secretary, Finance Department dated 4 December 1941, the State Archaeologist had suggested :

I am of the opinion that Khiching Museum does not require a highly paid Curator and if the present Curator is stationed there, his services cannot be utilised for the best interest of the State. If it is desirable that the post of the Curator should be abolished it may kindly be done. . . . .

Further he wrote

> I will require the assistance of Babu S.P. Bose always. It will not be possible for me to be present always at the field as there is none at the Headquarters to run the office. I can at best devote 3 weeks in the field and one week at the office. But this will not interfere in the carrying on of the excavation and conservation work as Babu S.P. Bose is fully qualified to manage the affairs during my absence.
>
> In order to do the excavation and conservation works I must have the assistance of the trained man and in our office Babu S.P. Bose is the only one upon whom I can put my reliance.

He proposed some archaeological work at Haripur and Viratgarh in 1942-43 simultaneously and suggested :

> The Curator of Khiching may kindly be transferred to Baripada towards

the end of March 1942

Accordingly, an order was passed on 5 April 1942 (Notification No. Est/G/3/120 dt. 5 April 1942).

In a special notification of the Finance Department the pay of Bose was raised to Rs. 150 P.M. "in consideration of his meritorious service". His duties were defined in another notification which stated that :

> S.P. Bose, Curator of the Baripāḍā Museum may take up the archaeological survey in the Sadar and Kaptipada Sub-divisions and the adjoining places in the Midnapore and Balasore districts, Nilgiri State during the period November 1942 to May 1943. He will visit all the important villages in a *parganah* or *pir* and collect information and write notes on each place bearing archaeological interest. He will go out of Headquarters for at least 20 days in a month from November 1942 to May 1943.[95]

From the Tour diary it is revealed that Bose was undertaking frequent tours to distant places despite his failing health. His letter to the State Archaeologist dated 21 November 1942 pointed out the great difficulties in visiting and searching archaeological sites. Everyday he was covering about 8 to 10 miles on cycle and 6 to 8 miles on foot. He felt concerned because the villagers were ignorant of the value of archaeological antiquities. He humbly prayed for an elephant to be arranged for his conveyance to carry out the survey works 'swiftly and efficiently'.[96]

Notwithstanding the problems mentioned above, Bose was able to survey Kuliānnā, Bangriposi and Sirsā area in the winter season. He reported about many stone images and ruined monuments in the area.[97] A copper-plate inscription was discovered from village Teltangia in Bāmanghāṭī Sub-division.[98]

All the works discussed above earned credit for Bose. The Director General of Archaeology had, in 1941, expressed happiness that the reconstruction work at Khicing had been completed and congratulated S.P. Bose for his efforts.

Despite all the good works undertaken by him in exploration, excavation and conservation of monuments in Mayūrbhañj, the State authorities did not appreciate his future plan of action for preserving the heritage. He had every reason to feel unhappy becuase the post of Curator of Khicing was abolished and he was transferred to Baripāḍā. He had taken pains to discover new chlorite stone quarry sites, and had trained the local people in stone cutting, stone masonry and temple building. By doing all these, he could restrict the expenditure in reconstructing the Great Temple and keep alive the tradition of stone work by the local artisans.[99] He was unhappy because 'no sympathy had been shown for the valuable services rendered by him to the cause of preserving art tradition of the State'.[100] Be that as it may, he alone could preserve the monuments of Mayūrbhañj for the posterity by giving them a new lease of life by adequate and timely conservation. He was in fact the Saviour of the cultural heritage of ancient Mayūrbhañj as manifested in her monuments and art.

The hypothesis that Khicing was the centre of a school of art in Orissā was first propounded by R.P. Candā. He had discovered the famous image of Hara which still adorns the local Museum with its spiritual serenity and artistic excellence. This image was supposed to be the tutelary deity of the Bhañja rulers for a long time before they adopted Khijjiṅgeśvarī-Cāmuṇḍā in that position. Candā's hypothesis was substantially corroborated by the discovery of several images and structural remains of shrines from Khicing. After the collections were exhibited in the local Museum, in Calcutta and London, the school gradually received recognition by the scholars like Rene Grosset of the Museum Gemme of Paris who discussed the subject in research journals and art publications.[101] Among India-based European scholars, Stella Kramrisch's views and appreciation of the art of Khicing highlighted the physical grace and charm of Khicing art. To her, the art represented a school with a new tradition as evidenced by the beautiful image of Mahiṣasurmardinī with its feminine charm and dynamism.[102] R.P. Candā's monograph *Bhanjas of Mayurbhanj and their Capital Khicing* served as a source book for the researchers working on eastern Indian art tradition for a long time. Though a part of the mainstream, the tradition of Khicing stood apart as a regional school of art in Orissā. The antiquity of Khicing art and architecture developed with a strong impact of

Kuṣāṇa art, because the origin of Khijjiṅgakoṭṭā (ancient name of Khicing) has been indisputably traced to the period of Kuṣāṇa rule. Its golden age was however in the time of the Bhañjas, i.e. ninth to eleventh centuries which witnessed large scale production of Brāhmaṇical, Buddhist and Jain art of outstanding quality, besides temples with early medieval characteristics.

These preliminary viewpoints of scholars found their full meaning when elaborate excavations and explorations were conducted by S.P. Bose during 1930-40. The discoveries made by him revealed the multi-dimensional nature of Khicing art. It would, therefore, be pertinent to make a selective study of the monuments and art objects which could be preserved by his efforts. The Great Temple which he had reconstructed during 1935-41 is at present a visible symbol of the ancient glory of Khicing. It was reconstructed with new stone blocks collected from the local quarries as well as old stones used in earlier temples. In its restored form the temple represents an Orissan *pañcaratha* type *vimāna* without the *jagamohana*. It is a typical *rekhā* structure showing five *pagas* (pillasters) i.e. one *rāhāpaga* at the centre, two *anurāhāpaga*s on either side of the *rāhāpaga* and two *konaka paga*s at the corners. These vertical projections on the outer face of the *vimāna* provide the structure both stability and grace. The sanctuary is square in ground plan, rectangular parallel piped from above the base with a curvilinear tower on top. There are three niches — one above the other on the outer faces of the temple, unlike Orissan temples elsewhere which have one niche each on the three sides to accommodate the *pārśvadevatā*s or *parivāradevatā*s. In the Great Temple, these niches are adorned with Gaṇeśa, Kārttikeya and Mahiṣasurmardinī. The iconographic features of these images resemble those of the deities found in the Brahmeśvara temple at Bhubaneśvar. Like the Brahmeśvara Temple, the original temple at Khicing appears to have been a *pañcāyatana* temple and the present Candraśekhara temple seems to be one of the four corner shrines.[103]

Both from architectural and sculptural points of view the Great temple of Khicing was a product of mature art and skill. Even in the restoration of the Candraśekhara and Kuṭaituṇḍi temples, the original plan was not altered in order to leave clear evidence of the architectural skill of the artisans for the future. A low *jagatī* was provided to all the three temples in their original form. In the front there is only one entrance with slight frontward projections. In the absence of *jagamohana* one may commit the mistake of grouping them with the Śatrughneśvara group of temples at Bhubaneśvar. But the vertical projections called *rathas* are indications of a later period of origin. Both vertically and horizontally they follow the Orissan tradition of temple architecture and there is no influence of any external tradition. Horizontally they are divided into several *bhūmis* and the *gaṇḍī* gradually recedes from the *baranda* to *grīvā* showing both symmetry and elegance. Finally, at the top, comes the huge *āmalaka* crowned by a *kalaśa* as a typical example of Orissan temple.

How Khicing faithfully preserved the Orissan tradition of art is also evident in the large number of sculptures recovered from the ruins. The presiding diety being Cāmuṇḍā or Khijjiṅgeśvarī, this illustrates the prevalence of Saptamātṛkā worship. Śāktism and Śaivism flourished simultaneously. The discovery of several Sūrya images prove the popularity of Sun-worship. In the Vedic mythology Rudra has been identified with the midday Sun. The worship of Rudra-Śiva, Hara, Umā-Maheśvara, Ardhanārīśvara and Liṅgam indisputably prove the unprecedented popular acceptance of the cult of Śaivism. Another cult in ascendance was that of Ganapati. There is a profusion of the images of Nāgas, Nāgins and Dikpālas. Several images of *Brahmā* with four faces and beard equally indicate the non-conventional acceptance of the Hindu deity.

The site called Itamuṇḍiā had been a rich Buddhist site and it yielded a number of images of Maricī. The place also yielded the inscribed pedestal of Avalokiteśvara and Buddha in the *bhūmiśparsa mudrā*. These and other images of Mañjuśrī and Tārā have been assigned to tenth-eleventh centuries. They not only bear testimony to the high quality of Buddhist art, but also to the strong appeal Buddhism had in Khicing. The discovery of Aparcana Mañjuśrī, Vajrāsana Buddha, Vajra Tārā and Kurukulla, etc. have tempted scholars like N.K. Sahu[104] to believe that Khicing was a centre of Tāntric Buddhism.

In the later period of Khicing, Jainism received wider popular support as known from the discovery of Jain Tīrthaṅkara images from the site called Chandiasal and in and around the Ṭhakurāṇī's compound. These Jain images have been identified with Ṛṣabhanātha, Pārśvanātha, Śāntinātha, etc.

While analysing the artistic merit of these sculptures one has to bear in mind the strategic location of Khicing at the converging point of trade routes passing between south Bihār and Orissā, Bengāl and Orissā, western Orissā and coastal Bengāl. This geographical knowledge has prejudiced some scholars to believe that Khicing art was a product of Gauḍīya influence or a synthesis between the Gauḍīya and Orissan school of art. R.P. Candā says:

> The regular features of these images of Khicing are a characteristic of the product of the schools of sculptures that flourished in Bengal and Bihar contemporaneously.[105]

It is, however, quite difficult to accept Candā's suggestion that the Bhañja rulers came from outside and they had engaged the artists of Bengāl and Bihār to produce Khicing art.[106] Stella Kramrisch was overwhelmed by the precision and metallic sharpness in carving and also in the emotional physiognomical expressions.[107] She compares the Pāla art with Khicing art of the Bhañjas. The remarks of Candā are hard to accept because (i) though most of the images of Khicing have the sensuous facial expression of Bengāl art, they do not have the same frankness or animated expression; (ii) the modelling of the the face differs; (iii) Khicing faces are oval, not longish and (iv) the standing images of Bengāl are more stiff than Khicing. The modelling of the body of the Khicing images is more smooth and elegant; their movements are more controlled. The Khicing images do not show the legs like stumps without vigour.

According to R.D. Banerjee there is a resemblance to the local type in the execution of faces and he calls this as the Oriyā type. These faces resemble the faces of the Oriyās living in the Garjat areas.[108] Stella Kramrisch too has observed this local Oriyā element in Khicing art in the 'amplitude of movement and largeness of modelling of the figures'.[109] She convincingly states that 'they establish a deeper rooted share of Orissan tradition'. Another eminent art historian Nihār Rañjan Ray also observes the Oriyā element in Khicing art "in the rare breath, fulness, and amplitude of modelling effecting into the sturdiness of form and appearance, executed further by their relative dimension".[110]

Balarām Śrīvāstav in a recent study of Khicing art comments :

> Decorative skill with metallic sharpness of the Pala style is visible in the rendering of the ornaments and other decorations of some figures, but this influence too is enriched by some amount of classical decorative elements such as the intricate 'kalpalatā' scrolls and arabesque designs. The carvers have aptly searched suitable occasions for such kind of rendering and have shown a remarkable skill in presenting the floral foliages and creepers encircling within them the 'Muktalobhi-hamsa', the 'Mithunas', the 'Pramathas', etc. Such elements bring the decorative treasure of Khiching art nearer to the classical decorative norms, and some of the carvings on the door jambs and other decorations are the real gems of Khiching art.[111]

With regard to the chronology of Khicing art the scholars have given different views and most of them associate it with the period of Bhañja rule. The absence of dated material makes the problem of chronology more complicated. A few inscription-bearing images do not provide any specific date. The Ādipur grant of Narendrabhañja alone refers to the year 193 of an era. If this is Bhauma era then the date is 193 + 736 = 929 AD. The Avalokiteśvara image bearing an inscription, which was discovered by K.P. Bose, has been assigned by N.K. Sahu to the eleventh century on the basis of palaeography[112] whereas Nāgendra Nāth Vasu[113] has assigned it to eleventh-twelfth century. According to R.P. Candā the Khiçing art flourished between eleventh and twelfth century.[114] But Kṛṣna Deva would like to put the image to tenth century AD.[115] N.R. Ray has assigned Khicing art to the tenth and eleventh century AD.[116] It would be probably wrong to consider Khicing art as dynastic art related to the Bhañjas alone. It would be more correct to interpret the art of Khicing as local art having a long period of evolution, efflorescence and decay. The whole range of Khiching art cannot be circumscribed to two centuries only. It must have taken a longer time to evolve, flourish and decline. On stylistic considerations, the art seems to have flourished from the ninth century to thirteenth century AD.

Though R.D. Banerjee has packed up the art of Khicing to eleventh-twelfth

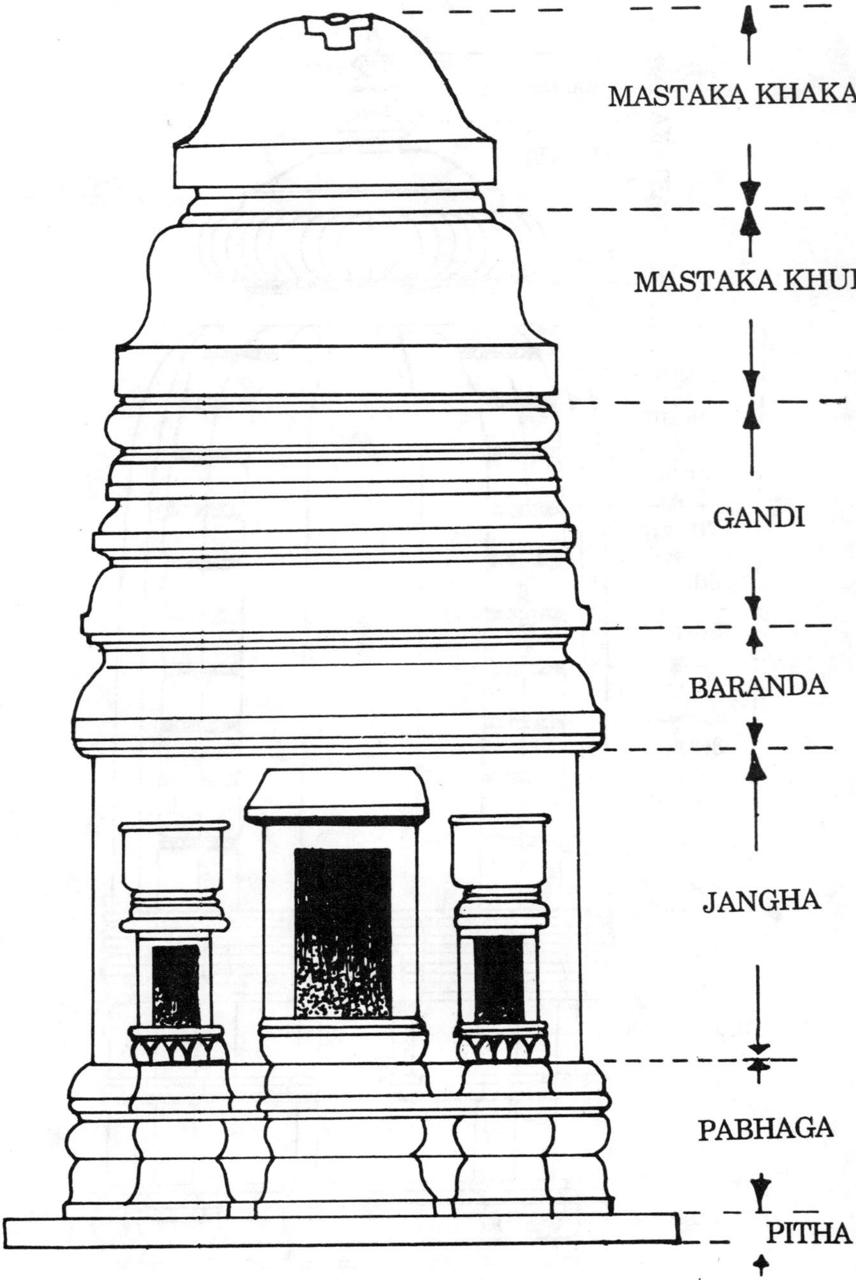

A typical *Khākāra* Temple of Orissa
(Courtesy: Archaeological Survey of India)

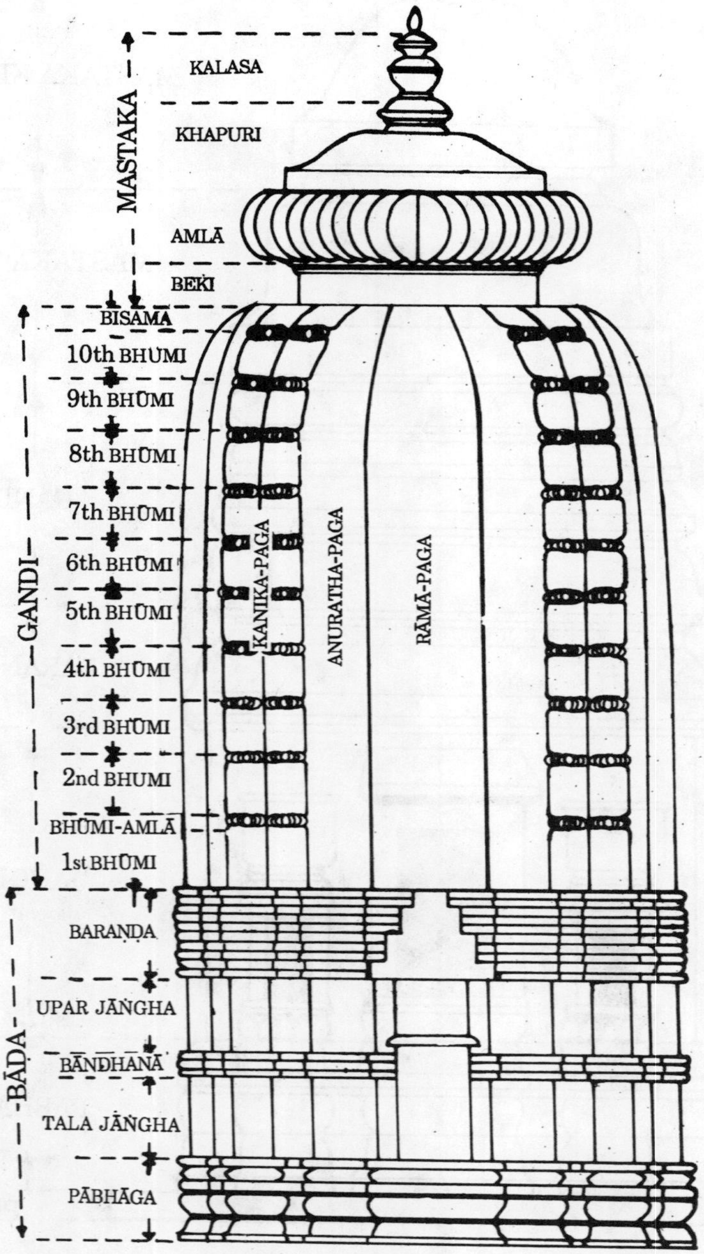

Principal components of a typically Orissan *rekha deula*
(Courtesy: Archaeological Survey of India)

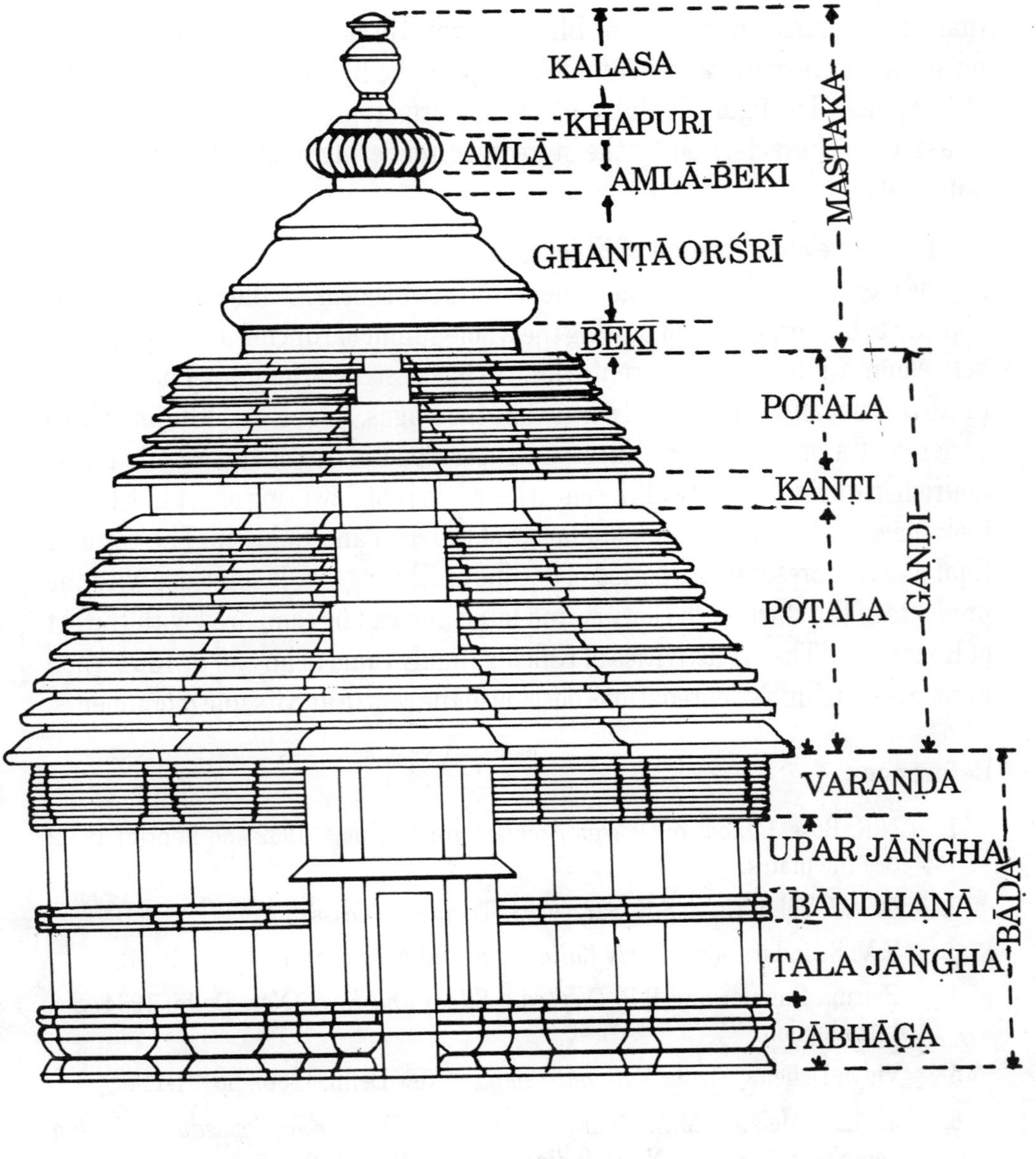

Principal components of a typically Orissan *pidha deula*
(Courtesy: Archaeological Survey of India)

centuries his classification of the art materials on stylistic ground appears reasonable.[117] He thinks that the Khicing art underwent three stages of evolution. Phase 'A' represented the earliest form of Hindu art, possibly older than the Mukteśvara temple of Bhubaneśvar. He has taken the door-jambs, meandering creepers, ornamental foliages and the figure of Hara as examples of this phase. The figure of Mahiṣamardini Durga represents the Phase 'B' and Phase 'C' is characterised by the stereotype rendering of objects which lacks naturality.

The above classification of Khicing art into three phases is acceptable, but not the idea of squeezing the phenomenon into two centuries. Balarām Śrīvāstav appears to be more sound in putting the whole gamut of Khicing art in the period between ninth to thirteenth centuries. He has assigned the First Phase to the ninth century AD when the local deities like the Nāgas, Nāgins and Khijjiṅgeśvarī underwent a process of acculturation. The Second phase or the Middle Phase flourished during tenth-twelfth centuries when real flowering of art in Khicing took place with the growing popularity of Śaivism and Śāktism. The third or final phase represents the period of decline of Khicing art. It coincides with the products of the thirteenth century and later, and can be compared with the art of Koṇārka.[118] The art activities of Khicing finally came to an end in 1361 when Feroz Śāh Tughluq's depredations destroyed the centre and its fine monuments.

References

1. N.K. Bose, *Canons of Orissan Architecture* (Calcutta, 1932 and Reprint 1982) *See* the plates.
2. *OHRJ*, Vol. I, No. 4, S.K. Saraswati, 'Temples of Orissa'.
3. K.V. Soundararajan, *Early Kalinga Art and Architecture*, (Delhi, 1984).
4. Bettina Baumer and R.P. Das (ed.), *Silparatna Kosa* (New Delhi, 1994) *See* Introduction.
5. Vidya Dehejia, *Yogini Cult and Temples* (New Delhi, 1986), pp. 91-114.
6. Michael Meister, M.A. Dhaky and Krishna Deva, *Encyclopaedia of Indian Temple Architecture* (North India) Chapters 18 and 19.
7. N.N. Vasu, *Archaeological Survey of Mayurbhanj*, Vol. I (Reprint, 1981), *See*

Preface.

8. *ASI*, 1922-23, pp. 124-28.
9. *Report published in ASI, Annual Report*, 1922-23, pp. 124-28.
10. *Mayurbhanj Information Bulletin*, July 7, 1946.
11. *ASI*, 1924-25, III, p. 13; A. Joshi, *op. cit.*, pp. 8-9; Report on the Administration of Mayurbhanj, 1923-24, p. 81.
12. *RAM*, 1923-24, p. 82, para 2.
13. *Ibid.*, 1926-27, pp. 109-11; *Ibid,* 1927-28, pp. 104-11.
14. Letter of Bose to P. Acharya, No. 4T dt. 15.6.1927.
15. File A(1) 1927-28 dt. 13 June 1927 (Z-20).
16. No. 8T dated 1 July 1927.
17. No. 11T, Karanjia, dt. 24 August 1927 and 12T, Karanjia, dt. 31 August 1927.
18. File No. B, 1935-36 dt. 19 February 1936.
19. File No. B, 1935-36, dt. 6 April 1935 Letter of P. Acharya, State Archaeologist to Dewan and Dewan to State Archaeologist No. 87 ED dt. 10 April 1935.
20. *Ibid.*
21. Mayurbhanj State Secretariat Notification No. Est/G/3/4514 D/14 September 1942.
22. *ASI*, 1922-23, pp. 124-28.
23. A. Joshi, *op. cit.*, p. 121. This information of Joshi is unfortunately not supported by any record.
24. A. Joshi reports in his thesis that the State Government incurred an expenditure of Rs. 15,000 in the above work. This appears incredible. (*Ibid.*, p. 121). Joshi further says the work was accomplished in 1928 (Page 9) which is wrong. P. Acharya in his work *Studies in Orissan History, Archaeology and Archives* has claimed that he dismantled the temples of Chandrasekhra and Kutaitundi and restored them from the bottom to the top. (Page 330). There is no Government record in support of this. On the contrary all records point out that the works of dismantling and reconstruction were done by S.P. Bose.
25. *Mayurbhanj Gazetteers*, (Oriya), October 1931 and *RAM*, 1931-32, pp. 110-12.
26. *ASI*, 1922-23, pp. 124-28.
27. Correspondence to the Dewan from P. Acharya, Examiner's Account, 1931-32, 1932-33.

28. *RAM*, 1930-31, p. 104 and *Ibid.*, 1932-33, pp. 108-09.
29. Report by S.P. Bose, Archaeological Supervisor, 25 March 1932; Also *RAM*, 1931-32, pp. 112-13; *Ibid.*, 1932-33, pp. 108-09.
30. State Archaeologists' Letter to Dewan dt. 1.7.1933.
31. Tour diary April 1932.
32. Tour diary August 1932.
33. *RAM*, 1923-24, p. 81; *ASI*, 1924-25, p. 13.
34. *RAM*, 1924-25, pp. 93-94.
35. *Ibid.*, 1928-29, pp. 107-09.
36. *Ibid.*, 1925-26, p. 99.
37. File 'B' 1933-34 dt. 1.7.1933, Z(28).
38. *Ibid.*, 25 April 1933, Z(29), Z(30). The 'New Temple' idea was mooted on 25 April with the consent of the maharaja who gave approval to purchase drawing materials on 1 July 1933.
39. *Ibid.*, dt. 5.2.1935, Z(23).
40. *RAM*, 1933-24, pp. 110-16.
41. *Ibid.*, p. 115.
42. File 'B' 1933-34 dt. 5 December 1934-Z(25).
43. Report of the Works 1934-35, S.P. Bose, Para-1.
44. *RAM*, 1934-35, p. 94.
45. P. Acharya to S.P. Bose, No. 72A dated 20.8.1932.
46. Letter to P. Acharya dt. 4.8.1933.
47. S.P. Bose to Dewan, Letter No. 240 dt. 5.2.1934.
48. *Ibid.*
49. File 'A' 1933-34, 10 April 1933 Z(140).
50. Letter No. 6T B dt. 16.7.34 S.P. Bose to Dewan.
51. File B-1935-36 dt. 22.8.34 and *RAM*, 1935-36, p. 113.
52. *RAM*, 1935-36, p. 113.
53. S.P. Bose' Note to State Archaeologist and the latter's Note to Dewan dated 4 January 1935, File 'B' 1935/36 dt. 4.1.35 and 4.5.1935.
54. *RAM*, 1936-37, p. 91.

55. *Ibid.*, 1937-38, pp. 100-101.
56. *Ibid.*, 1938-39, pp. 88-89.
57. Letter to the State Archaeologist dt. 15.9.1935.
58. File 'A' 1936-37 Letter from State Archaeologist to the Curator dt. 3.12.36.
59. Letter No. 25A dt. 12.9.1937.
60. State Archaeologists' letter to P.K. Das, Assistant Secretary to Government dated 21.12.1939.
61. Bose to H.H. the Maharaja dated 1 December 1936.
62. Mayurbhanj State Gazette, May 7, 1938, Notification dated 19 April 1938.
63. D.O. No. 1295 dated 13 February 1939 from D.G. Archaeology to Paramananda Acharya, Mayurbhanj State.
64. D.O. No. 1122-20-3403 New Delhi dated 30 April 1941.
65. Bose to State Archaeologist No. 68K dt. 8 September 1940.
66. *RAM*, 1941-42, pp. 117-19.
67. *Ibid.*, 1930-31, pp. 104-09.
68. *Ibid.*, p. 108.
69. P. Acharya, *op. cit.*, pp. 533-37.
70. *RAM*, 1930-31, pp. 105-9.
71. *Ibid.*, 1931-32, pp. 110-14.
72. *Ibid.*, p. 115.
73. *Ibid.*, 1933-34, pp. 110-11.
74. Devala Mitra, *Ratnagiri*, Two vols. (1981); C. Fabri, *History of the Art of Orissa*, 1974, pp. 33-63.
75. P.K. Mishra, Survey and Documentation of Monuments in the Upper Mahanadi Valley (Unpublished Report), Sambalpur University, 1995.
76. N. Senapati (ed.), ODG-Mayurbhanj, pp. 57-58.
77. N.K. Sahu, *Utkal University History of Orissa*, Vol. I, (1964), pp. 413-60; and E.J. Rapson, *Indian Coins,* p. 25.
78. Snigdha Tripathy, *Early and Medieval Coins and Currency System of Orissa* (1986), pp. 35-57.
79. *RAM*, 1933-34, pp. 112-13.
80. *Ibid.*, p. 113.

81. *Ibid.*, p. 116.
82. *Ibid.*, 1934-35, p. 94.
83. *Ibid.*, 1937-38, pp. 101-02.
84. *Ibid.*, 1938-39, p. 87.
85. *Ibid.*, p. 90.
86. *Ibid.*, p. 90.
87. *Ibid.*, 1941-42, p. 117.
88. *Ibid.*, 1939-40, p. 131.
89. N.K. Sahu, *op. cit.*, pp. 440-41.
90. D.O. No. 1295 dt. 13 February 1939 from K.N. Dikshit, Director General of Archaeology in India to Paramananda Acharya, Superintendent of Archaeology, Mayurbhanj State.
91. K.C. Panigrahi, *Autobiography* (in Oriya) 1987, p. 29.
92. *RAM*, 1943-44, p. 148.
93. *Ibid.*, 1945-46, p. 192.
94. *Ibid.*, p. 171.
95. Mayurbhanj State Secretariat Notification Est. G/3/4514 dt. 14.9.1942.
96. Letter dated 21 November 1942.
97. *RAM*, 1942-43, p. 139.
98. *Bhanjapradipa* 1348 SE,p. 20.
99. Letter of Bose to the Secretary, General Department, dated 3 September 1941.
100. *Ibid.*
101. Quoted by P. Acharya, *Studies in Orissa History, Archaeology and Archives*, p. 381.
102. *Indian Sculpture*, pp. 112, 194.
103. For further details, *see* T.E. Donaldson, *Hindu Temple Art of Orissa*, Vol. I, pp. 239-41. The learned author is, however, wrong to state that the restoration work had commenced in 1925.
104. *Buddhism in Orissa*, 1958, pp. 212-14.
105. R.P. Candā, *op. cit.*, pp. 29-30.
106. *Ibid.*, p. 30.
107. *Inidian Sculpture*, p. 116.

108. *History of Orissa*, II, p. 329.
109. *Indian Sculptures*, p. 116.
110. R.C. Majumdar (ed.), *Struggle for Empire*, p. 651.
111. *The Art of Khiching*, New Delhi, 1986, p. 14.
112. N.K. Sahu, *op. cit.*, p. 213.
113. *Archaeological Survey of Mayurbhanj*, p. LXXVII.
114. *Bhanja Dynasty of Mayurbhanj*, p. 4.
115. B. Srivastav, *op. cit.*, p. 16.
116. R.C. Majumdar (ed.), *Struggle for Empire*, p. 651.
117. R.D. Banerjee, *op.cit.*, p. 397-99.
118. R.D. Banerjee, *op. cit.*, pp. 17-18.

4

Epilogue

AMONG several sites of historical interest in Orissā, Khicing enjoys a conspicuous position. Mayūrbhañj was the first state where the Department of Archaeology was set up much earlier than other princely states. Orissā was not a separate province till 1936 and the Commissioner of Orissa Division had no responsibility with regard to the monuments of the feudatory states. Even the Archaeological Survey of India did not extend its protective interest over the archaeological sites located in the princely states. The Rājās of Mayurbhañj being liberal and enlightened had understood the value and significance of ancient sites having monuments. They took care to obtain the services of eminent Indologists like Nāgendra Nāth Vasu, Ramā Prasād Candā, and Rākhāldās Banerjee to study the antiquities of Mayūrbhañj. Though it was motivated by their desire to search for the identity of the Bhañja dynasty, the outcome was quite meaningful so far as the discovery of the monuments was concerned. Mayurbhañj earned fame while attracting the attention of scholars for the large deposits of palaeolithic and neolithic tools of Kuliānā, Baidipur and Kuchai, etc. which added new information on India's prehistoric civilisation. In the historic period, the discovery of punch-marked coins, Kuṣāṇa and Purī Kuṣāṇa coins, and Gupta coins provided a new dimension to Orissan culture. Where monuments were concerned, the fame of Khicing and Haripur spread far and wide by archaeological explorations conducted by K.P. Bose and N.N. Vasu in the first decade of the present century. The establishment of a regular department of Archaeology in the time of Mahārāja Pūrṇa Candra Bhañj Deo and the direct collaboration of experts of the Archaeological Survey of India ushered a new era in archaeology in Mayūrbhañj which had a direct bearing on the culture and civilisation of ancient Orissā.

Though the State Department of Archaeology consisted of the State Archaeologist and Archaeological Supervisor at the beginning (1927), in course of time it functioned from three centres, viz. Baripāḍā, Haripur and Khicing and the designation of the Supervisor was changed to Curator (1935). While Paramānanda Ācārya remained the State Archaeologist (1927-49) the post of Supervisor and later Curator was consecutively held by Śailendra Prasād Bose. Ācārya, being a science graduate, took great interest in geology and prehistory. He also had special interest in studying archival records for which the state government had deputed him to work in the India Office Library, London; Bengal Secretariat Record Room at Calcutta and the Secretariat Record Room at Rāṅcī. Apart from the study of records he supervised the activities of the Department as and when necessary. This is evident from his own correspondence as well as from the remarks of the Mahārāja quoted below as an extract from the File on the Annual Administration Report for 1933-34.

> He (P. Acharya) visited Khiching when it was necessary for him to inspect the work and instruct the Archaeological Supervisor on the spot while Babu S.P. Bose, the Supervisor conducted all the works done at Khiching during the year under report. The Supervisor deserves credit for conducting the excavation at Biratgarh which was done with care. He also gave particular attention to the collection of materials for the construction of the New Temple.
>
> (Dewan's Office Memo No. 1847 E dated Baripada 23 November 1934)

The above note of the Dewan was endorsed by the Maharaja who gave his views as, "Yes, his (Bose's) work is very creditable".

Even Ācārya had admitted in his numerous correspondence that he was least available at the Headquarters for day-to-day administration owing to his involvement in record collection and the services of S.P. Bose were indispensable to him. From 1927 when Bose joined as the Archaeological Supervisor his main duty was conservation, exploration and excavation. He spent more than three years at Haripur town, the medieval capital of Mayurbhañj, in excavating the ruined palace and monuments followed by careful conservation work. To him excavation and conservation were of equal importance. He was so deeply engrossed with the work that he could overcome the distance and many other hazards of living at Haripur. He had no formal training in archaeological works. But he could make up the deficiency by dint of hard labour and a spontaneous eagerness to learn. His diary reveals that during spare time he found pleasure in reading books on history. He always maintained a library, a part of which he used to carry to Transit Camps. He developed knowledge on flora, fauna and mineral wealth of India and was prompted to write articles on 'The Wealth of India'. This and many other popular articles on historical sites of Mayūrbhañj show his flare for writing. His English and Oriyā articles show that lucidity and coherence were his hallmarks. He was a good photographer and draftsman besides being an artisan who made various tools required for fishing and sculpture on stone. He also sculpted images and various articles for domestic use. That he was a good musician having mastery over playing harmonium and semi-classical music is borne by the fact that the Mahārājā, a good *tabalcī* himself, used to have several sessions with his archaeologist friend. From various sources it is known that he was a private music teacher of the Rānī of Bastar (married to a cousin brother of the Maharaja of Mayūrbhañj) who had presented him with a costly harmonium having golden reeds. That music provided him with sustenance during his lonely sojourn in archaeological camps is reported by the labourers and workers who had the opportunity to work with him at Khicing and other places. They also reveal that in weaving textiles and pisciculture Bose had adequate knowledge. He had trained hundreds of stone cutters and masons at Khicing while reconstructing the Great Temple during 1935-1942 in order to keep the cost of construction low. He preferred the local masons to those brought from Bhubaneśvar because he wanted to revive the ancient stone work of Khicing so that the trained local people would be able to earn their livelihood by adopting a noble profession. After the completion of the Temple he took steps to arrange for their resettlement at workshops near Keshna and Baripāḍā. Some of the octogenarians trained by him still remember him with nostalgic memory for the professional guidance he had given them.

From the Autobiography of K.C. Pāṇigrahī we come to know that those days Khicing and the adjacent area (Sulkruli, Raruan, etc.) was full of dense forests. Even in day time wild beasts used to roam around the villages. After night fall human movement was rare. Life was forlorn, isolated and unbearable. It is incredible how a sophisticated person like Bose with his family could live for 15 long years under such circumstances where neither educational nor health and hygiene problems could be encountered easily. His muted reactions to the environment found expression through letters to friends. It was sheer love for work and dedication to duty coupled with a spirit of challenge that helped him to overcome all adverse situations. Eye witnesses recollect that to tide over monotony he organised music sessions in the evenings. At times he transcripted Bengālī drama in Oriyā to be played by the local artists as *yātrā*. He could organise a well-knit *yātrā* party for periodic entertainment and relaxation. His love for sports became evident when he organised football teams and tournaments with local youths. To overcome the problem of health and hygiene he learnt homeopathy and administered doses to afflicted persons for immediate relief. His wife was a mother figure to all and sundry taking care of expectant mothers. She served as a midwife when the first child of K.C. Pāṇigrahī was born. It was quite natural for the local people to respect Bose as a great benefactor of the community. By uncommon zeal and perseverence he not only recovered the precious antiquities but also reconstructed a temple which symbolised the pride and heritage of the people. His career is a brilliant example of a man's doggedness to acquire knowledge and determination to achieve the goal. In him one may find the spark of Kāmākṣa Prasād Bose, the pioneer archaeologist of Mayūrbhañj, gradually turning into smouldering fire without which the monuments of Mayūrbhañj would have been totally jeopardised and obliterated. The temples of Candraśekhara, Kuṭaituṇḍi and Khijjiṅgesvarī could be successfully retrieved by him from the jaws of complete annihilation. The above temples, the Site Museum at Khicing and the well-preserved Rasikrāya temple at Haripur are the silent witnesses to his unstinted devotion to archaeology and culture. With his Midas' touch, he could galvanise dead stone into life; and with his enviable qualities of head and heart, he could endear himself to the people, an incredible achievement for a man whose involvement in the Terrorist movement of Bengāl in the post-partition days would probably have led him to the gallows.

In 1942 S.P. Bose joined the Headquarters of the State Department of Archaeology as Curator of Baripāḍā Museum. His transfer from Khicing was most unexpected. The type of job satisfaction that Khicing could provide him was not to be found anywhere else. He was suddenly confronted with the stark realities of bureaucratic machination. The transfer was tantamount to the removal of a successful General from his loyal command. He wished to settle down at Khicing with those simple tribal folks with whom he had worked for fifteen long years, treating them as members of his family and encouraging them to adopt the creative profession of sculpturing stones and building temples. He had discovered a quarry of serpentine-stone in the inaccessible jungles of Jaśīpur which he wanted to prospect for commercial purposes to provide the artisans with new opportunities for earning their livelihood. But his dreams did not come true. Instead of feeling happy over the transfer to Baripāḍā, he took it as an order of exile.

The year 1944-45 was a critical period for the State monarchy. Under the aegis of the Prajāmaṇḍal the popular movement had taken a new turn intensifying peasant unrest against the feudal social order. The approaching reality of freedom for India and transfer of power by the British authorities to Indian leaders had put the ruling prince in a quandary. The political turmoil was likely to engulf the princely order in utter annihilation. Under the circumstances nothing could be done to assuage the feelings of Bose notwithstanding the Mahārāja's personal liking for him. In 1944 he was elected to the Prajāsabhā (State Council) of Mayūrbhañj. Though his aim was to serve the people and the State as a loyal citizen in a period of unprecedented crisis, Providence had decided otherwise. While in the Jaśīpur jungle prospecting the serpentine-stone quarry he caught fever and had to be shifted to Baripāḍā for treatment. He was a diabetic patient and for diabetes, in those days, suitable medicine was not available. The medical treatment was not adequate to save his precious life and he passed away on 17 July 1946, leaving behind his wife and six children in acute economic distress. His premature death at the age of 47 cast a gloom over the elite community of Baripādā and the people with whom he had worked as a family at Khicing and Haripur. The condolence resolution passed by the Mayūrbhañj Prajāsabhā on 9 September 1946 while paying eloquent tribute to the departed soul said:

> Though Birbal Babu is dead and gone yet he lives amidst us in the monuments of art and architecture that he recreated and left behind to stand witness for ages to come . . . .

His death was an irreparable loss to archaeology — a void which has not been filled up till this day.

Today one remembers his dedication to archaeology while witnessing the historic monuments which he had saved from the brink of destruction. The atmosphere at Khicing and Haripur is so much surcharged with his loving memory that a visitor can easily see the footprints of Bīrbal Bābū (as he was popularly known) on the sands of time. The people of Khicing still cherish his memory as a father figure. Though his contributions to Orissan archaeology has not been given due recognition by scholars till now, the standing monuments — the lone sentinels of his work — bear witness to his lifelong dedication to the cause of archaeology. They silently shed tears for their saviour; but for whose indefatigable zeal and care there would have been no trace of the proud heritage.

Postscript

THE preceding chapters have been devoted to a survey of the archaeological activities in Mayūrbhañj during the period of the British Raj. It was under the director-generalship of Sir Mortimer Wheeler (1944-48) that scientific archaeology and new methods of excavation were introduced in India. Krushna Chandra Panigrahi who had been deputed to the Archaeological Survey of India for intensive training in the new methods of field archaeology, did not return to state service as he preferred to join the Government of India. After Independence the Mahārājā of Mayūrbhañj handed over the state administration to a popular Government headed by Premier Sarat Chandra Das, the Prajāmaṇḍal leader. During 1947-48 the popular Government of Das was besieged with many problems like political and cultural isolation and tribal uprising for merger with Bihar. Unable to cope with the crisis created by the armed rebellion of the tribals, Sarat Chandra Das transferred the state administration to the Government of India. After a brief rule by the central government, Mayūrbhañj merged with the province of Orissa on 1 January 1949.[1] Consequently, the State Department of Archaeology was abolished and its rich library was shifted to Bhubaneśvar to constitute the Orissa State Museum Library. Paramānand Ācārya, the State Archaeologist was transferred and appointed as the Superintendent of Orissa State Museum with headquarters at Bhubaneśvar. In the following pages we shall examine the progress of work done in Mayūrbhañj in various aspects of archaeology in the post-1947 period.

Prehistory

Despite the apathy of the state government the vast archaeological potentialities of Mayūrbhañj, however, did not go unnoticed. In 1948 N.K. Bose and Dharani

Sen of Calcutta University conducted an excavation of the Stone Age sites in Mayūrbhañj.[2] The result of their further research was published in *Man in India* in 1958.[3] One of the most painstaking scholars who made significant contributions to promote the study of Indian prehistory in the sites of Mayūrbhañj was G.C. Mahapatra of the Deccan College of Poona.[4] He discovered a number of new sites (listed in Appendix)[5] which added new information to the nature and extent of the prehistoric Culture in North Orissa. His explorations in 1957-58 brought to light six sites in Pañcapīr and Bāmanghāṭī Sub-divisions where tools of Series II were totally absent, probably due to the non-availability of raw materials like jasper, chert and chalcedony. However, tools of Series I were found in abundance at Kuliānā, Mahuliā and Pratāppur. Some of the tools of Series II showed a microlithic tendency.[6] Simultaneously, D. Mittra and D.K. Chakravarty of the Archaeological Survey of India collected a large number of neolithic tools from known sites of Baidyapur, Kuchāi, Āmsikrā, Marudā and Silipuñji in the Sadar Sub-division. Mittra also found a large number of microliths including parallel sided blades and lunates made of chert and flint. Chakravarty collected four neoliths and numerous microliths from neighbouring areas of Bara Mandā, and Radiābandh. Sites like Pratāppur, Haripur and Madhupur yielded some neolithic tools.[7]

The gap between the prehistory and early history of Orissa is now being gradually bridged with the discovery of more stone shouldered and metal celt sites. Pure metal celt sites were reported from Khiciṅg, Kṣetra, Bāghrā and Bāghdāpīr in Mayūrbhañj and Dunriā in Dhenkanāl district. In Baripada Museum some copper implements have been preserved. They have been obtained from Bāmanghāṭī and Pañcapīr Sub-divisions. The Khiciṅg specimens are two shouldered celts and that of Kṣetra belong to the bar celt type. The specimen from Bāghdā is a massive double edged battle axe measuring one and half feet in length. A hoard of 10 copper tools from Bāghrāpīr were recovered from one foot below the surface on the bank of the Gulpha river. Many of these are of double edged battle axe variety. Their thickness varies from 1/8 to 1/20 of an inch. The largest among them is 18½ inches long and 15¾ inches wide; the smallest being 10-1/3 inches long and 7 inches wide. In view of the typology of the finds from Khiciṅg, Pañcapīr and Bāmanghāṭī area and the stratigraphy of the Bāghrāpīr deposit, these celts are of great value. But no study has yet been made on the technique of their manufacture.[8]

In 1961-62 B.K. Thapar of the Archaeological Survey of India undertook an exploratory dig at Kuchai, a known neolithic site near Baripāḍā, to investigate the assemblage of the eastern neolithic culture. The excavated artefacts from the upper deposit were of the butt and variety. The neolithic artefacts clearly showed the use of the grinding and polishing technique. These were found together with a coarse grit tempered red ware and an orange brown ware.[9] From the lower deposit microliths of non-geometric industry were found. The types included blades, points, lunates and scrappers.[10]

Ashok Kumar Ghosh and A.N. Basu of the Department of Anthropology, Calcutta University revisited Baripāḍā and Kuliānā in 1968-69 to make fresh observations on the sections and tool assemblages.[11]

In the recent years a new trend in archaeological research has prompted the scholars to enter the domain of ethno-archaeology for which Mayūrbhañj provides ample scope. Kishore K. Basa of the Department of Archaeology, Utkal University has broken new grounds in this.[12]

Inscriptions

The history and the genealogy of the Bhañjas of Khijjiñga *maṇḍala* is based on the following Copper-Plate Inscriptions.[13]

Bāmanghāṭī Plate of Raṇabhañjadeva
Khaṇḍadeuli Plate of Raṇabhañja
Copper Plate of Raṇabhañja
Ādipur Copper Plate of Narendrabhañja
Keśarī Cooper Plate of Śatrubhañja
Bhañja Grant of Khicing
Bāmanghāṭī Plate of Rājabhañja
Ukhuṇḍa Plate of Pṛthvībhañja
Charter of Ra(?)bhañjadeva
Ādipur Copper Plate of Durjayabhañja

All the charters except the last one, were issued from Khijjiṅga-koṭṭa. Though the language of the inscriptions is Sanskrit, most of the texts are erroneous. They invariably mention a *Saṁvat* with reference to Bhauma era (AD 736). Apart from the origin of the Bhañjas there is reference to the genealogy and titles of various officials. The seal is a full blown lotus containing the figure of a couchant bull facing a trident with a crescent over it. There are several place-names helpful in reconstructing the historical geography of the period. Among the above-mentioned copper plates the Khaṇḍadeuli Plate was first read by Kāmākṣyā Prasād Bose in August 1916 which helped Hara Prasād Śāstrī in editing the same in Vol. IV, Pt. II of the *Journal of Bihar and Orissa Research Society* (June, 1918). The preliminary reading of Bose, the Deputy Collector, is quoted below :

> This plate is of Copper and in shape like a spade. It has a copper medallion on the top and in it are in bas-relief a Swastika, a bull and a goddess. The letters are of late *Kutila* kind and resemble Bengali and Oriya letters. Its size is 9 inches long and 7 inches broad.[14]

Although the Bhañjas had issued all their charters from Khijjiṅgakoṭṭa only one was recovered during excavation from the Ṭhakurāṇī compound at Khiciṅg, by Śailendra Prasād Bose, the Curator in December 1941, and it was preserved in Baripada Museum. In 1948 Paramānanda Ācārya sent it to Dinesh Chandra Sircar for editing. Sircar published it in the *Epigraphia Indica*, XXX , pp. 220-25. This is a single copper plate measuring 8½"x7" with a circular seal on top. The lower end of the seal is designed in the form of an expanded lotus with a couchant bull. Above the bull the inscribed legend reads — (1) *Śrī Mahada (?) bhañja devasya*. The next in Sanskrit is full of errors and some words are beyond recognition. Though Sircar finds the script to be of the 'Gauḍiya type' Snigdha Tripathy accepts it as 'Proto Oriya'. The *Saṁvat* is not clearly legible. The name of the donor is read as Śrī Mohanmadahavabhañja, son of Śrī Ranabhañja and the donee's name is mentioned as Kālaśarmā, son of Pālaka.[15]

In 1952 Paramānanda Ācārya, the then Superintendent of Research and Museum, Bhubaneśvar gave to Satyanārāyaṇa Rājguru, the epigraphist, a few estampages of three Stone Inscriptions preserved in the Baripada Museum.

These Inscriptions were earlier collected by Kāmākṣyā Prasād Bose from Peḍāgaḍi in Udalā (Kapṭipadā Sub-division of Mayūrbhañj) and measured

No. 1 : 13" x 3"

No. 2 : 13" x 3"

No. 3 : 13½" x 4"

Each Inscription contains three lines of writing; No. 1 and 3 are in prose and No. 2 is in verse. The language is Sanskrit but the script belongs to different periods — ranging from the ninth to the eleventh centuries. Rājguru is of the opinion that the stone slab was the portion of a pillar erected either inside the temple or temple compound so as to attract the attention of the visitors. This explains the possibility of the text being inscribed at different periods of time and thus, the variation in the script.

The Inscriptions are records of grants made in favour of certain deities by the following persons : (1) Kumāra Dharmarāja *alias* Durgarāya; (2) Satr̥bhañjadeva and (3) Dhr̥varāj Deva. There is no reference to their identity/ status. The grants were made in favour of God Pinākapati, Līleśabhadrā and Bharadi in fulfilment of the desires of the donors. This is an indication of the popularity of Śaivism and Śāktism on account of royal patronage.[16]

Numismatics

Mayūrbhañj was often cited by the numismatists for the discovery of Punch-marked Coins,[17] Roman Coins,[18] Puri-Kuṣāṇa Coins,[19] Gupta Gold Coins,[20] Gaṅga Fanams, Gajapati Pagoḍās,[21] and Muslim Coins[22] giving thereby a continuous history of the currency system which prevailed in the Bhañja kingdom. In 1962-63 a hoard of 192 pieces of Punch-marked coins was collected from Baripāḍā for the Orissa State Museum. The coins have not been brought to the notice of the public till now.[23] Since the Punch-marked coins represent the earliest coinage of India which enjoyed wide circulation as legal tender, their discovery in Mayūrbhañj is an indication of brisk commercial activities and an efficient exchange system of a vigorous economy.[24]

On the abundant availability of Purī-Kuṣāṇa coins several scholars have supported the theory of Kuṣāṇa rule over Orissa.[25] In 1948 one thousand two hundred and sixty seven Purī-Kuṣāṇa Coins along with a single copper coin of Kaniṣka were found at Bhañjakīa.[26] In 1956 twelve coins of the above type were collected from a brick mound at Ḍerā near Kuliānā and handed over to the Orissa State Museum for preservation. These are yet to be published.

The earliest discovery of Gupta Gold coins in Orissa was reported from Mayūrbhañj in 1939 from a village called Bhānpur in the Kapṭipadā sub-division. Though there was a big hoard, only three could be recovered. These belong to the famous Archer type of coins issued by Emperor Candragupta II. In Indian numismatics the Gupta Gold coins occupy a place of profound importance for their abundance, beautiful execution and artistic design. Their discovery from Mayūrbhañj and other places led to the speculation that Gupta rule had prevailed in Orissa. The use of Gupta era in some Orissan epigraphs substantiated the theory of Gupta rule.[27] Scholars also believe that the port of Tāmraliptī was connected with Vārāṇasī through a land route which passed through Khijjiṅgamaṇḍala and South Kośala, and was frequented by traders and pilgrims.[28]

Monuments and Sculpture

Besides the monuments discussed in the preceding pages (Chapters 2 and 3), Mayūrbhañj boasts of other temples representing the Orissan style of architecture. Among the Rekhā temples mention may be made of Kakhāruā Baidyanāth Temple at Mānitri and Jagannāth temple at Baripāḍā. The builder of Kakhāruā Baidyanāth Temple was Prince Kakhāruādeva, the son of Gajapati Pratāparudradeva (AD 1497-1533).[29] The temple has two adjuncts, i.e., the *Jagamohana* and the *Naṭamandira* and the latter one was built by Rājā Jadunāth Bhañja. The Jagannāth Temple at Baripāḍā was the work of Rājā Baidyanāth Bhañja. An inscription gives its date as 1497 SE, i.e., AD 1575. Inside the temple premises there are many small cells housing deities of Jainism and Buddhism. A number of Jain *Tīrthaṅkaras*, Avalokiteśvara, Jambhala and Umā-Maheśvara images adorn these cells. These images were obviously collected from other places and accommodated in the Jagannāth Temple for preservation and security. Both the above temples are of identical design. The ruined Pāśa-Caṇḍī temple at Baḍasāhi was made of *Bhadrā* design. This Śākta temple was 21'6" in height and it can be assigned to the sixteenth century. During the fifteenth century the Gauḍīya style of temple architecture had made inroads into Mayūrbhañj on account of its close proximity to Bengal. Therefore, besides the Rasika Rāya and Rādhāmohan temples of Haripur, the famous Ambikā temple at Baripāḍā also seems to have followed the Gauḍīya tradition. It appears that Mayūrbhañj not only provided a congenial atmosphere for the growth of Brāhmaṇical and heterogeneous faiths, but also accepted Orissan and Gauḍīya traditions of temple architecture.[30]

An account of several other places having ruined structures and monuments of Mayūrbhañj is provided in R.P. Mohapatra's *Archaeology in Orissa*, Vol. II (1986), pp. 137-61. Among these places important are Baḍasāhi, Devagrāma, Kiśorepur, Kośalī, Koisārigarh, Mānitri, Pratāppur, and Peḍāgaḍi, besides Baripāḍā, Haripur and Khiciṅg. While the vestiges of Śakti Worship are available at Baḍasāhi, Devagrāma, Khicing, Kiśorepur, Koisārigarh, Kurariyāgarh, and Peḍāgaḍi, Jainism seems to have had its strongholds at Baripāḍā, Khiciṅg, Kośalī, and Khuntapal. Numerous sculptures of great aesthetic value and iconographic interest have been recovered from these places. Some of the art objects are now preserved in the Museum at Baripāḍā and in Khiciṅg. Nabin Kumar Sahu's *Buddhism in Orissa* (1959), pp. 212-14, brought to limelight some excellent Buddhist sculptures of Mayūrbhañj. There are sites like Somivrkṣa and Virāṭgarh which are mentioned in the *Mahābhārata* episodes. In the Medieval period several forts were constructed for strategic reasons and their ruins can be seen even today at Baḍa Belakunti, Dubigarh, Haripur, Īṭāgarh, Kusumiā, Kurariyāgarh, Koisārigarh, Pathuriāgarh and Rāṇibandha. It would be no exaggeration to say that Mayūrbhañj is an archaeological paradise and the gateways to its fascinating wealth were flung open during the Durbar administration by the pioneering works of Kāmākṣyā Prasād Bose and his son, Śailendra Prasād Bose.

References

1. D.M. Praharaj, *Tribal Movements and Political History of India* (1988), pp. 156-68.
2. N.K. Bose and D. Sen, *Excavation in Mayūrbhañj*, Calcutta University (1948).
3. Geological and Cultural Evidences of the Stone Age in Mayūrbhañj, *Man in India,* 38, pp. 49-55.
4. *The Stone Age Culture of Orissa* (1962).
5. *See* Appendix-A.
6. *Indian Archaeology 1957-58*, A Review, p. 41.
7. *Indian Archaeology 1958-59*, A Review, p. 38.
8. G.C. Mohapatra, *op.cit.*, pp. 41-46.
9. B.K. Thapar, *Recent Archaeological Discoveries in India*, Paris (1985).
10. *Indian Archaeology 1961-62*, A Review, p. 36.
11. *Indian Archaeology 1968-69*, A Review, p. 25.
12. Pre-history of Mayūrbhañj, A Review; Un-published M.A. dissertation, 1984 and Ethnoarchaeology of Orissa, A Review, in *Man in Society*, 6, pp. 79-106.
13. Snigdha Tripathy, *Inscriptions of Orissa*, VI, pp. 1-48.
14. *JBORS*, IV, Pt. II, p. 172.
15. S. Tripathy, *Inscriptions of Orissa*, VI, pp. 30-33.
16. *OHRJ*, Vol. I, No. 2, July 1952, pp. 178-80.
17. *RAM*, 1928-29, pp. 104-07; This year's numismatic finds included Purī-Kuṣāṇa Coins, Silver Coins and Coins with Arabic and Persian legends.
18. J.D. Beglar's account published in the *Report of the Archaeological Survey of India 1874-75 and 1875-76*, pp. 72-73 and Quoted by P. Acharya in *Journal of Numismatic Society of India* II (1940).
19. *Annual Report of the Archaeological Survey of India 1924-25*, p. 38; *Indian Culture* III, pp. 727-30; *RAM*, 1933-34, pp. 112-13. The first hoard of Purī-Kuṣāṇa coins was found at Bhañjakiā in 1923. In 1924-25 the second hoard was found at Birātgarh during excavation. In May 1939, 105 Purī-Kuṣāṇa Coins were discovered in a brass container from Village Manada. A hoard of 282 Copper Coins including 112 genuine Kuṣāṇa Coins came to the notice of R.D. Banerjee, *History of Orissa*, I, pp. 111-15. Besides the above hoards there were other small discoveries too.
20. Three Gold Coins of Candragupta II were discovered at Bhānpur in August 1939; *RAM*, 1933-34, pp. 110-16; 1933-40, pp. 130-35 and 1943-44, pp. 144-49.

See JNSI cited above.

21. *RAM*, 1928-29, pp. 107-09. Five gold coins representing Fanams and Pagoḍās were found along with Purī-Kuṣāṇa Coins from Birāṭgarh area by S.P. Bose.

22. One small Copper Coin of Alāuddīn Hussan Shāh of Bengal; 27 large and 11 small Silver coins of Shāh Ālam, Last Mughal Emperor, were found. *RAM*, 1930-31, pp. 104-11; 7 Silver Coins of Shāh Ālam, *RAM*, 1945-46, p. 171.

23. S. Tripathy, *Early and Medieval Coins and Currency System of Orissa* (1986), p. 5.

24. Their date varies from 1000 BC to fourth century BC. Cunningham, *Coins of Ancient India*, p. 43; S.K. Chakraborty, *Ancient Indian Numismatics*, p. 33.

25. N.K. Sahu, *History of Orissa*, I, pp. 413-60.

26. *OHRJ*, II, p. 85.

27. For further discussion *see* G.S. Patel, *History and Culture of India* (1992), pp. 23-24.

28. S. Tripathy, *op.cit.*, (1986), pp. 67-68.

29. The sister of Gajapati Pratāprudra was married to one Jagannāth Bhañja of Mayūrbhañj who received Baripāḍā Dandapat as dowry.

    P. Mukherjee, *History of the Gajapati Kings of Orissa* (1953), p. 99, fn. 200.

30. N. Senapati, *Orissa District Gazetteer — Mayūrbhañj* (1967), pp. 56-57.

Appendix

Sites of Early Stone Age :

Āmsikrā	Do-muhānī	Malichā
Banspal	Ghanṭśilā	Mundabanī
Bārāsol	Kuliānā	Mendhakhai
Baripāḍā	Kuchai	Nuāberi
Bangiriposi	Kamarpal	Pratāppur
Bijatala	Koilisnta	Patiñja
Bisoi	Kamtā	Pariākolī
Brāhmaṇgāon	Kalabariā	Sandim
Buramara	Kendudihā	Sirsā

Bhuāsuni	Mahuliā	

Site of Middle Stone Age :

Badra	Bijatala	Bisoi
Bahaldā	Bonāikalā	Kandaliā
Bārāsol	Barmaṇḍā	Rairaṅgpur

Sites of Microliths :

Badra	Bonaikālā	Rairaṅgpur
Bisoi	Maṇḍa	

Sites of Polished Stone Celts :

Āmsikrā	Bonāikalā	Haripur
Basipitha	Chitrada	Indipur
Amdalisasan	Dahikuṭhī	Jadipal
Baidīpur	Dukurā	Jaipur
Khama	Maṇḍa	Pratāppur
Kapṭipadā	Maruda	Radiābandha
Kuchai	Madhupur	Ura Chandbilā
Khiciṅg	Naraharipur	

Sites of Soldered Celts :

Āmsikrā	Baidīpur	

Sites of Neolithic Pottery :

Baidīpur

Sites of Copper Celts :

Bāghrāpīr	Khetra	Bāmanghāṭī
Pañcapīr	Khiciṅg	

Source : Appendix to Chapter I 'Pre-history' by G.C. Mahapatra in N.K. Sahu, Utkal University, *History of Orissa*, Vol. I (1964), pp. 55-56.

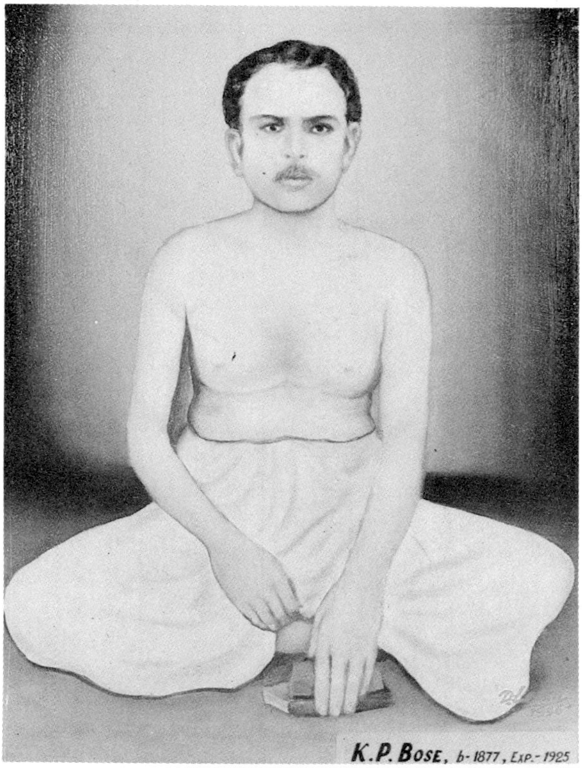

Pl. 1 Kamaksha Prasad Bose.

Pl. 2 Sailendra Prasad Bose
— Birbal Babu.

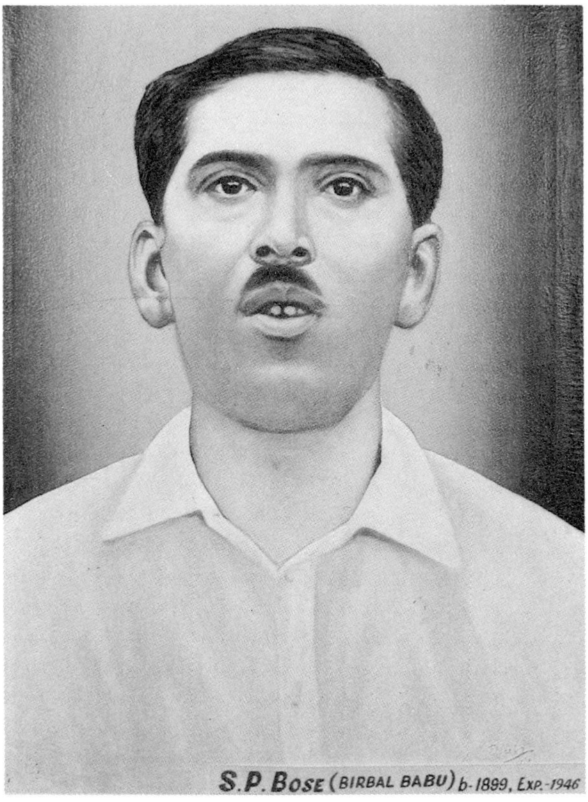

Pl. 3 Ṭhakurāṇī's Compound before the temple was built, Khicing.

Pl. 4 Caulkuṅjī monolithic pillars, Khicing.

Pl. 5 Kīcakeśvarī temple, Khicing under construction during Governor's visit in 1938-39.

Pl. 6 Constructing Kīcakeśvari temple, Khicing up to plinth level in 1936-37.

Pl. 7 Kīcakeśvarī temple, Khicing under construction.

Pl. 8 Kīcakeśvarī temple, Khicing (present status).

Pl. 9 Candraśekhar temple, Khicing — before renovation.

Pl. 10 Candraśekhar temple, Khicing — after renovation (present status).

Pl. 11 Kutaituṇḍi temple, Khicing — before renovation.

Pl. 12 Kutaituṇḍi temple, Khicing — after renovation (present status).

Pl. 13 Rasikrai temple, Gaudia style, Haripur.

Pl. 14 Terrakotta work at Rasikrai temple, Haripur.

Pl. 15 S. P. Bose on flower-bed at Haripur during its excavation in 1927-28.

Pl. 16 Umā-Maheśvara, Khicing.

Pl. 17 Sūrya, Khicing.

Pl. 18 Viṣṇu, Khicing.

Pl. 19 Śiva, Khicing.

Pl. 20 Pārśavanāth, Khicing.

Pl. 21 Brahmā, Khicing.

Pl. 22 Nṛsiṁha, Barsāhī.

Pl. 23 Gaṇeśa, Khicing.

Pl. 24 Dhyānī Buddha, Khicing.

Pl. 25 Tārā — Goddess of Lotus, Khicing.

Pl. 26 Brahmāṇī, Khicing.

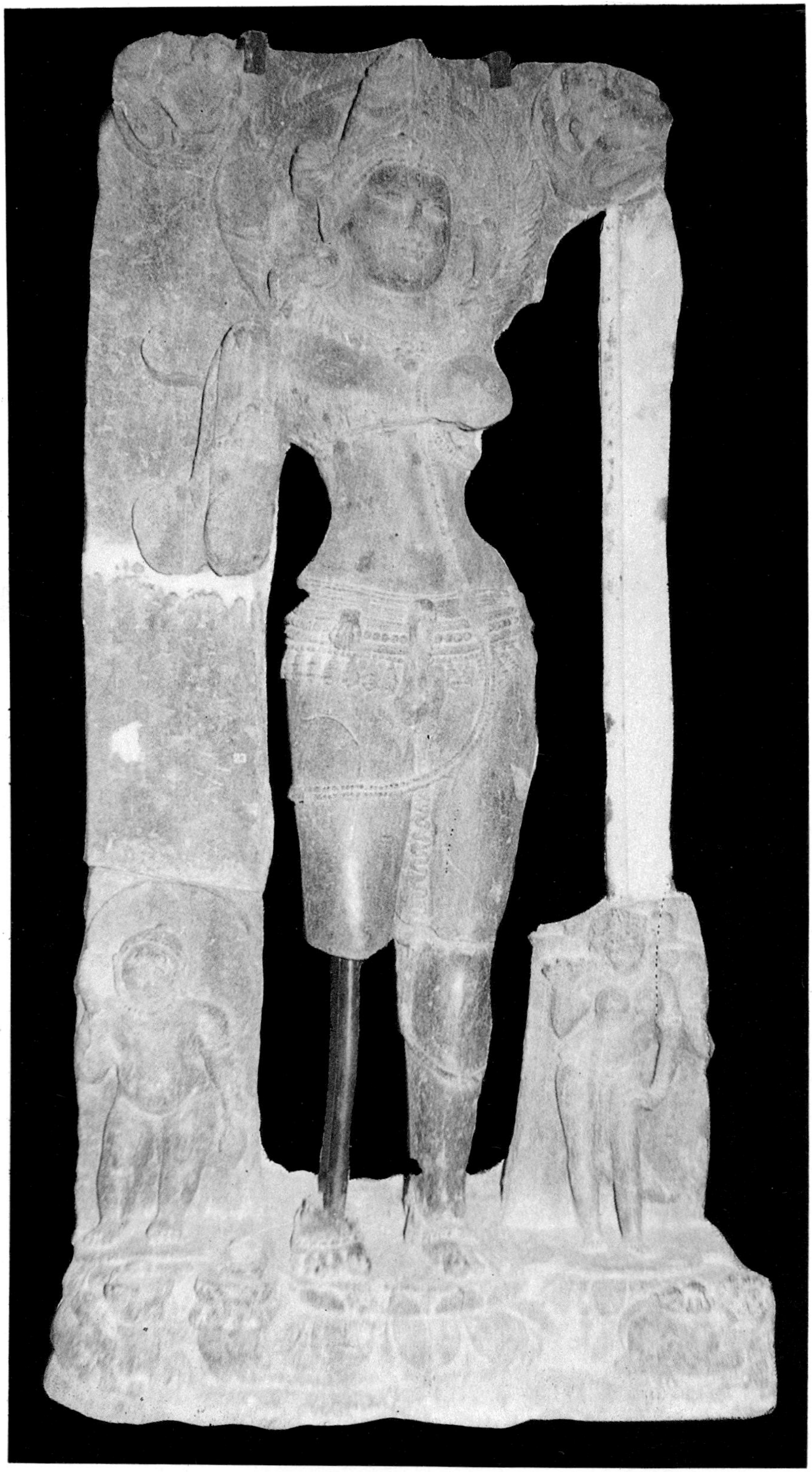

Pl. 27 Ardhanārīśvara, Khicing.

Pl. 28 Avalokiteśvara, Khicing.

. 29 Upāsikā, Khicing.

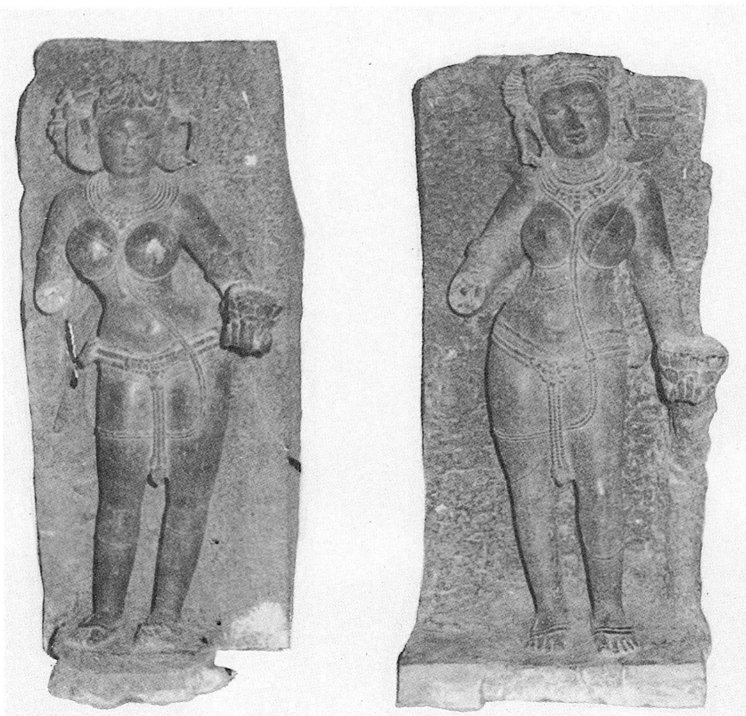

Pl. 30 Nāga, Khicing.

Pl. 31 Nāga-stambha — Naga-pillars, Khicing.

Pl. 32 Maricī, Khicing.

Pl. 33 Marīcī, Udala.

Pl. 34 Bodhisattva, Khicing.

Pl. 35 Stone inscription of Dhrubarāja Deva, Kaptipāḍā sub-division.

Pl. 36 Bhairava, Khicing.

Pl. 37 Garuḍa, Ageriā.

Pl. 38 Varāha, Ageriā.

Pl. 40 Dhyānī Buddha, Khicing.

Pl. 39 Nāga, Kuamāra in Kaptipāḍā sub-division.

Pl. 41 Broken Image of Umā-Maheśvara, Kainsarigarh.

Pl. 42 Mahiṣaśurmardinī.

Pl. 43 Avalokiteśvara, Podadihā, near Udala.

Pl. 44 Ajaikapada,
Kaptipāḍā sub-division.

Pl. 45 Model of a temple made by
S. P. Bose and Bansidhar Naik.

. 46 Table top
ade of granite
stone by S. P.
Bose.

Pl. 47 Art objects made of serpentine and granite stone by S. P. Bose.

Pl. 48 Decorative Sculpture
made of serpentine stone
by S. P. Bose.

Pl. 49 Garuḍa
made of granite stone
by Govinda Sahu —
a mason trained by
S. P. Bose.

Appendix

List of the Masons of Khicing Since the year 1935

Sl. No.	*Names of Masons*	*Sl. No.*	*Names of Masons*
1.	Bansidhar Naik	23.	Birisana Naik
2.	Chutu Naik	24.	Gora bhuyi
3.	Akaya Naik	25.	Bharmara Naik (Ulaikundi)
4.	Mangloo Naik		
5.	Nisa Naik	26.	Nandu Mahakud
6.	Lal Mohan Naik	27.	Bharmara Naik
7.	Sukudev Sahu	28.	Sira Naik
8.	Shreedhar Naik	29.	Govinda Sahu
9.	Kruha Mohakud	30.	Dasarathi Naik
10.	Manu Naik	31.	Jagannath Behera
11.	Panu Giri	32.	Ghasiram Behera
12.	Surendra Sahu	33.	Gopinath Sahu
13.	Kahil Sahu	34.	Nalu Patra
14.	Rusinath Sahu	35.	Rangadhar Sahu
15.	Braja Mohan Sahu	36.	Magia Naik
16.	Akadusia Giri	37.	Thalamoni Naik
17.	Somanath Naik	38.	Dola Barik
18.	Bhagaban Naik	39.	Haldhar Naik
19.	Kailash See	40.	Kartik Naik
20.	Panchanna Sahu	41.	Pitambar Behera
21.	Bhakta Charan Sahu	42.	Brusara See
22.	Charan Behera	43.	Purusotam Sahu

Sl. No.	*Names of Masons*
44.	Acha Rauta
45.	Bhima Ghadai
46.	Sira Ghadai
47.	Brunda Behera
48.	Mahasur Mohanty
49.	Ram Hari Ghadai
50.	Sukadev Giri
51.	Daitari Barik
52.	Mohan Giri
53.	Kailash Giri
54.	Ratnakar Behera
55.	Upendra See
56.	Daitari Giri
57.	Kamal Lochan Giri
58.	Bansidhar Giri
59.	Udhab Giri
60.	Dhanu Barik
61.	Kulamani Naik
62.	Bhanu Naik
63.	Bharmara Sahu
64.	Daitari Giri (Kasipal)
65.	Daitari Sahu
66.	Baga Deo
67.	Subarna Deo
68.	Pitabas See
69.	Sindhu Naik
70.	Sudarsan Patra
71.	Sanatan See
72.	Dibakar Bhui
73.	Sankar Giri
74.	Gaja Giri
75.	Shreepati Deo
76.	Biranchi Ghadai
77.	Dhanasur Behera
78.	Bauju Khatua
79.	Bhikari Behera
80.	Murali Sahu
81.	Bhanja Sahu
82.	Narotom Sahu
83.	Arjun Sahu
84.	Lokanath Sahu
85.	Ramachandra Sahu
86.	Suka Behera
87.	Narsing Behera
88.	Lilambar Behera
89.	Khatra Behera
90.	Dibakar Behera
91.	Pravakar Behera
92.	Ghana Sham Behera
93.	Sau Sira Naik
94.	Bhadru Naik
95.	Dibakar Giri
96.	Dinabandhu Khatua
97.	Jogendra Sahu
98.	Bhagirathi Naik
99.	Ankul Ghana
100.	Balara Naik

Bibliography

Gazetteers, Reports, Journals and Bulletins

Ancient India (1949)

Annual Report of the Archaeological Survey of India

Archaeological Survey Reports

Arts Asiatique (1957)

Files from the Mayūrbhañj Collectorate Record Room

Indian Antiquary (1928)

Indian Archaeology, A Review

Indian Historical Quarterly (1939)

Journal of Asiatic Society of Bengal

Journal of Bihar and Orissa Research Society (1927)

Journal of Orissan History

Journal of Royal Society of Arts (1933)

Kalinga Historical Research Journal

Mayurbhanj Gazetteer

Marg (1955 and 1958)

Mayurbhanj Information Bulletin

Memoirs of Archaeological Survey of India, No. 44 (1930)

Memoirs of the Numismatic Society of India

Modern Review (1911 and 1930)

New Aspects of History of Orissa

Orissa Historical Research Journal

Reports on the Administration of Mayurbhanj

The Imperial Gazetteer of India

Books

Acharya, P., *Studies in Orissan History, Archaeology and Archives*, Cuttack, 1960.

———, *Notes on Archaeological Sites and Temple at Khicing* (Mayurbhanj Gazette).

———, *Archaeological Operation in Khicing*, (Mayurbhanj Gazette, 1931).

Banerjee, R. D., *History of Orissa*, Vols. 1-2, Calcutta, 1930.

Beglar, J.D., *Archaeological Survey of India Report*, 1974-76.

———, *Report of Tours in the Southeastern Province in 1874-75 and 1875-76*, Calcutta, 1882.

Behera, K.S., *Temples of Orissa* (1983).

Bettina Baumer, *Silparatnakosa* (1994).

Boner Alice, Sharma, *Silpa Prakasa* (196).

Bose, N.K., *Canons of Orissan Architecture* (1932).

Bose, N.K. and Dharani Sen, *Excavation in Mayurbhanj* (1948).

Chanda, R.P., *Explorations in Orissa, Memoirs of Archaeological Survey of India*, Calcutta, 1930.

——, 'Notes on the Ancient Monuments of Mayurbhanj', in *Journal of Bihar and Orissa Research Society*, 1927, Vol. XIII.

——, *Bhanja Dynasty of Mayurbhanj and their Ancient Capital, Khicing* (1929).

Chattopadhyay, B., *The Age of the Kuṣāṇas — A Numismatic Study* (1979).

Cobden, Ramsay, L.E.B., *Feudatory States of Orissa* (Reprint, 1981).

Dash, Ghanashyam, 'Puspagiri Mahavidyalaya', in *Jhankar* VI (1953).

Dehejia, Vidya, *Early Stone Temples of Orissa* (Delhi).

——, *Yogini Cult and Temples* (1986).

Fabri, C.L., *The History of Art of Orissa* (1975).

Ganguly, M.M., *Orissa and Her Remains* (1912).

Joshi, Arjun, *History and Culture of Khijjingakotta*.

Mahtab, H., *History of Orissa* (Oriya).

Mohapatra, R.P., *Archaeology in Orissa*, 2 Vols. (1986).

——, *Jain Monuments in Orissa* (1984).

Maiti, S.K., *Early Indian Coins and Currency System* (1970).

Majumdar, B.C., *Orissa in the Making* (1925).

Majumdar, R.C., *Age of Imperial Kanauj*.

——, *Struggle for Empire*.

Mishra, P.K. (ed.), *Comprehensive History and Culture of Orissa*, Vol. I (1996).

Mishra, P.K. (ed.), *Culture, Tribal History and Freedom Movement* (1987).

Mishra, P.K., *Political History of Orissa* (1900-1936), 1979.

Mitra, D., *Bhubanesvar* (ASI, 1958).

——, *Ratnagiri* (ASI, 1981).

———, *Bronzes of Achyutaragpur,* Delhi, 1978.

Mitra, R.L., *Antiquities of Orissa I and II* (Reprint, 1963).

Orissa Sahitya Akademi, *Art Traditions of Orissa* (1983).

Patel, S.K., *Cultural History of Early Medieval Orissa* (1981).

Panigrahi, K.C., *Archaeological Remains of Bhubanesvar* (1961).

———, *History of Orissa* (1981).

Praharaj, D.M., *Tribal Movements and Political History of India* (1988).

Ramachandra Rao, C.V., *Administration and Society in Medieval Andhra* (1976).

Rowland, B., *The Art and Architecture of India* (1977).

Sahu, N.K., *Buddhism in Orissa* (1958).

———, *History of Orissa I* (1964).

Sahu, N.K., *et al., History of Orissa.*

Sahu, N.K. (ed), *New Aspects of History of Orissa* (1970).

Sarkar, S.N., *Biography of Maharaja Sreeram Chandra Bhanj-deo* (1918).

Saraswati, S.K., *Survey of Indian Sculpture* (1962).

Senapati, N., *Orissa District Gazetteers — Mayurbhanj* (1969).

Sivaramamurty, C., *Indian Painting.*

Srivastav, Balaram, *The Art of Khicing* (1986).

Tripathy, Snigdha, *Inscriptions of Orissa,* VI (1974).

———, Early *and Medieval Coins and Currency System of Orissa* (1986).

Vasu, Nagendra Nath, *Archaeological Survey of Mayurbhanj* (1911).

Index